THE CONSTITUTIONAL RIGHT TO A SPEEDY AND FAIR CRIMINAL TRIAL

Recent Titles from Quorum Books

Retail Marketing Strategy: Planning, Implementation, and Control
A. Coskun Samli

Venturing Abroad: Innovation by U.S. Multinationals
Frank Clayton Schuller

Microcomputers, Corporate Planning, and Decision Support Systems
The WEFA Group, David J. Gianturco, and Nariman Behravesh, editors

The Investment Side of Corporate Cash Management
Robert T. March

A Practical Approach to International Operations
Michael Gendron

Exceptional Entrepreneurial Women: Strategies for Success
Russel R. Taylor

Collective Bargaining and Impasse Resolution in the Public Sector
David A. Dilts and William J. Walsh

New Directions in MIS Management: A Guide for the 1990s
Robert J. Thierauf

The Labor Lawyer's Guide to the Rights and Responsibilities of Employee
Whistleblowers
Stephen M. Kohn and Michael D. Kohn

Strategic Organization Planning: Downsizing for Survival
David C. Dougherty

Joint Venture Partner Selection: Strategies for Developed Countries
J. Michael Geringer

Sustainable Corporate Growth: A Model and Management Planning Tool
John J. Clark, Thomas C. Chiang, and Gerard T. Olson

Competitive Freedom Versus National Security Regulation
Manley Rutherford Irwin

Labor Law and Business Change: Theoretical and Transactional Perspectives
Samuel Estreicher and Daniel G. Collins, editors

THE CONSTITUTIONAL RIGHT TO A SPEEDY AND FAIR CRIMINAL TRIAL

WARREN FREEDMAN

Q QUORUM BOOKS

New York · Westport, Connecticut · London

Library of Congress Cataloging-in-Publication Data

Freedman, Warren.
The constitutional right to a speedy and fair criminal trial /
Warren Freedman.
p.   cm.
Bibliography: p.
Includes index.
ISBN 0-89930-331-5 (lib. bdg. : alk. paper)
1. Speedy trial—United States.   2. Fair trial—United States.
3. Due process of law—United States.   I. Title.
KF9223.4.F74   1989
345.73′056—dc19
[347.30556]   88-15391

British Library Cataloguing in Publication Data is available.

Library of Congress Catalog Card Number: 88–15391
ISBN: 0-89930-331-5

First published in 1989 by Quorum Books

Greenwood Press, Inc.
88 Post Road West, Westport, Connecticut 06881

Printed in the United States of America

The paper used in this book complies with the
Permanent Paper Standard issued by the National
Information Standards Organization (Z39.48-1984).

10 9 8 7 6 5 4 3 2 1

Contents

Preface

The timely importance of the subject matter of the speedy and the fair criminal trial is attested to by simple reference to today's headlines, not only in the press but in all media, particularly television. The public at large is very familiar with the constitutional right to a speedy and fair criminal trial. The TV medium, in particular, has shown numerous classics written by the great English novelist Charles Dickens who portrayed so vividly the languor of English prison life in the last century. Indeed, modern investigating reporters employed by the media search out those instances where defendants have a long stay in prison while awaiting trial; these same investigators monitor the criminal trials to assure that fair trials are commonplace. In the final analysis, it is the bench and bar that are the vigilantes to assure the criminal defendant his constitutional right to a speedy and fair trial.

The author acknowledges that the time expended in writing this volume was made possible by the understanding of his family: his dear wife Esther, a psychiatric social worker; his son, Dr. Douglas Freedman, an orthodontist; his daughter Miriam, a New York City senior art director for a large advertising agency; and his daughter Debbie Freedman Stiebel of Avon, Connecticut, a renowned primary school teacher, and her husband Michael Stiebel, a practicing attorney.

1

Background to the Speedy and the Fair Criminal Trial

1.1 INTRODUCTION

Professor Wilkinson in his 1974 study "Serving Justice" (at page 146) opined that "criminal rights is probably the area of the U.S. Supreme Court's work that is most prone to emotional reaction, either one of sympathy for a disadvantaged suspect or of outrage at the perpetrator of a violent crime." Professor Graham opined in his 1970 study, "The Self-Inflicted Wound" (at page 4), that "history has played cruel jokes before, but few can compare with the coincidence in timing between the rise in crime, violence and racial tension in the United States and the U.S. Supreme Court's campaign to strengthen the rights of criminal suspects against the State." These two opinionative views of the criminal justice system simply point up the necessity for close adherence to the constitutional guarantees concerning the speedy trial and the fair trial.

The Sixth Amendment to the U.S. Constitution provides that "in all criminal prosecutions, the accused shall enjoy the right to a speedy and public trial." The thrust, as pointed out in United States v. MacDonald,[1] is to minimize the possibility of long incarceration before trial, to reduce impairment of the liberty of the accused while released on bail, and to shorten disruption of life caused by arrest for a criminal matter. The Sixth Amendment also minimizes anxiety accompanying public accusation and limits impairment of the defense resulting from any long delay.[2] The Sixth Amendment affords criminal defendants the right to trial by an impartial jury drawn from the state and the district in which the defendant allegedly committed the crime.[3]

The Fifth Amendment to the U.S. Constitution, pursuant to its due process clause, provides that "no person shall be . . . deprived of life, liberty, or property without due process of law," and thus protects, for example, defendants against intentional and prejudicial preaccusation delay.[4]

Several federal statutes like the Speedy Trial Act of 1974,[5] the Interstate Agreement on Detainers Act of 1970,[6] and the Federal Rules of Criminal Procedure[7] protect defendants, for example, from undue post-accusation delay.[8]

It should be observed that the right to a speedy trial, while guaranteed by the Sixth Amendment, is made applicable to the states by the Fourteenth Amendment.[9] As expressed by the U.S. Supreme Court in Dickey v. Florida,[10] "the right to a speedy trial is not a theoretical or abstract right, but one rooted in reality in the need to have charges promptly exposed."

The guarantee of the fair trial is also delineated by the Sixth Amendment's insistence upon a public trial and is further enforced under the procedural guarantees of equal protection of the law and of due process of law under the Fourteenth Amendment.[11]

The U.S. Constitution itself also bears upon the issues of speedy and of fair criminal trial; for example, under Article I, Section 8, Congress

shall have the Power . . . to constitute Tribunals inferior to the supreme court . . . to define and punish Piracies and Felonies committed on the high Seas, and Offenses against the Law of Nations . . . and to make all Laws which shall be necessary and proper for carrying into Execution the foregoing Powers, and all other Powers vested by this constitution in the Government of the United States, or in any Department or Officer thereof.

Article III delineates the "judicial power," Article IV describes the Full Faith and Credit that must be given "in each State to the public Acts, Records and judicial Proceedings of every other State," and Section 2 thereof states that "the Citizens of each State shall be entitled to all Privileges and Immunities of Citizens in the several States."

Freedom of the press under the First Amendment also bears heavily upon the issues of speedy and fair trials, as perhaps evidenced by the recent appellate court decision in New York Times Co. v. Demakos.[12] Here the press brought a proceeding to prohibit the court from excluding the press and the public from the criminal courtroom and to compel the court to release the transcript of any plea proceedings involving the criminal defendant. At the outset of the per curiam opinion the New York Appellate Division, 2nd Dept., found that the trial court's action

"in precluding the public and the press from plea proceedings is improper. . . . The courts have consistently held that the right of the public and press to attend court proceedings, civil and criminal, is guaranteed by the Federal and State Constitutions (US Const, 1st Amend; NY Const, art I, §8; see, Globe Newspapers Co. v. Superior Ct., 457 US 596; Richmond Newspaper v. Virginia, 448 US 555; Gannett Co. v. DePasquale, 443 US 368; Matter of Capital Newspapers Div. of Hearst Corp. v. Moynihan, 71 NY 2d 263; Matter of Westchester Rockland Newspapers v. Leggett, 48 NY 2d 430; Matter of Herald Co. v. Weisenberg, 89 AD 2d 224, affd 59 NY 2d 378; see also, Judiciary Law §4 ["The sittings of every court within this state shall be public, and every citizen may freely attend the same"]). In criminal cases, the right of access has been extended not only to the trial itself, but also to pretrial hearings (see, Press-Enterprise Co. v. Superior Ct., 478 US —, 106 S Ct 2735; Waller v. Georgia, 467 US 39; Matter of Associated Press v. Bell, 70 NY 2d 32), voir dire proceedings (see, Press-Enterprise Co. v. Superior Ct., 464 US 501), and plea proceedings (see, Matter of Hearst Corp. v. Clyne, 50 NY 2d 707).

"In cases dealing with the claim of constitutional right to access to criminal proceedings, the courts have recognized that open-court proceedings serve several purposes.

"First, 'contemporaneous review in the forum of public opinion' (Matter of Oliver, 333 US 257, 270) serves to protect the accused from 'secret inquisitional techniques' and unjust persecution by public officials and 'goes far toward insuring him the fair trial to which he is entitled' (People v. Jelke, 308 NY 56, 62) . . . The public also has an interest in seeing that there is justice for the accuser—the police and the prosecutors who must enforce the law, and the victims of crime who suffer when the law is not enforced with vigor and impartiality. And when justice has been done, public awareness 'serve[s] to instill a sense of public trust in our judicial process' (People v. Hinton, 31 NY 2d 71, 73) by assuring the innocent and impressing the guilty with the power of the rule of law. Justice must not only be done; it must be perceived as being done" (Matter of Westchester Rockland Newspapers v. Leggett, 48 NY 2d 430, 437, supra).

In Press-Enterprise Co. v. Superior Court (464 US 501, 508, supra, quoting from Richmond Newspapers, Inc. v. Virginia, 448 US 555, 570, supra), the Supreme Court also noted that the open trial "has what is sometimes described as a 'community therapeutic value.' " The court further explained:

"Criminal acts, especially violent crimes, often provoke public concern, even outrage and hostility; this in turn generates a community urge to retaliate and desire to have justice done . . .

"When the public is aware that the law is being enforced and the criminal justice system is functioning, an outlet is provided for these understandable reactions and emotions. Proceedings held in secret would deny this outlet and frustrate the broad public interest; by contrast, public proceedings vindicate the concerns of the victims and the community in knowing that offenders are being brought to account for their criminal conduct by jurors fairly and openly selected" (Press-Enterprises Co. v. Superior Court, 464 US 501, 508–509).

This is not to say that a criminal proceeding may never be closed to the public or press. It has been recognized that the right to an open trial may give way in certain instances to other rights or interests, such as an accused's right to a fair trial or the government's interest in avoiding the disclosure of sensitive information. However, closed proceedings must be rare and may only be held for cause shown which clearly and compellingly outweighs the value of openness (see, Waller v. Georgia, 467 US 39, 45, supra; Matter of Westchester Rockland Newspapers v. Leggett, 48 NY 2d 430, 438, supra). The Supreme Court set forth the applicable rule in Press-Enterprise Co. V. Superior Court (464 US 501, 510, supra):

"The presumption of openness may be overcome only by an overriding interest based on findings that closure is essential to preserve higher values and is narrowly tailored to serve that interest. The interest is to be articulated along with findings specific enough that a reviewing court can determine whether the closure order was properly entered" (see also, Globe Newspaper Co. v. Superior Ct., 457 US 596, 606–607, supra; Matter of Westchester Rockland Newspapers v. Leggett, supra, at 442).

Prior to deciding whether closure of court proceedings is warranted, the Trial Judge must provide the interested parties with notice and an adequate opportunity to be heard on the issue (see, Matter of Westchester Rockland Newspapers v. Leggett, supra, at 442). Moreover, a court's decision to close a criminal proceeding to the public and the press may not be based upon conclusory assertions but must be supported by specific factual findings (see, Press-Enterprise Co. v. Superior Court, 478 US—, 106 S Ct 2735, 2741–44, supra).

1.2 POWERS OF THE U.S. SUPREME COURT OVER CRIMINAL COURTS

The U.S. Supreme Court's supervisory powers over the federal courts and also state courts is not limited to the enforcement of constitutional guarantees, but encompasses "the duty of establishing and maintaining civilized standards of procedure and evidence."[13] The U.S. Constitution and amendments thereto are designed to curb the power of the federal government, and, in theory, the state courts, which, for example, are free to carry out their own notions of speedy trial, fair trial, or other aspects of criminal justice,[14] the Fourteenth Amendment reasserted the power of the highest court over state courts by its provision that no state could "deprive any person of life, liberty, or property, without due process of law." Thus, the U.S. Supreme Court was vested with responsibility over the caliber of state criminal justice. The Fourteenth Amendment's due process clause expresses a demand for standards of fair procedure perhaps not defined under other amendments.[15]

The due process clause of the Fourteenth Amendment, as enforced particularly by the U.S. Supreme Court, prohibits state courts resorting to methods that violate those rights "so rooted in the traditions and conscience of our people as to be ranked as fundamental."[16]

The highest court has also been responsible for developing a coherent standard for determining when a violation of the U.S. Constitution during a criminal prosecution may constitute "harmless error."[17] It was in 1919 that Congress had codified the "harmless error" rule,[18] but almost fifty years later in Chapman v. California[19] the U.S. Supreme Court held that not all constitutional violations required the automatic reversal of a trial verdict because some errors are "in the setting of a particular case . . . so unimportant and insignificant" that they may be deemed "harmless" beyond a reasonable doubt.[20] Interestingly, the 1967 opinion of the highest court proclaimed that certain rights like the right to counsel,[21] the right to an impartial judge,[22] and the right to be free from coerced confession,[23] could never be treated as "harmless error."[24] In 1986 in Delaware v. Van Arsdall[25] and in Rose v. Clark[26] the court ruled that violations of both the right to cross-examine a testifying witness and the right to instruct properly the jury can constitute "harmless error."[27] Yet in 1973 in Davis v. Alaska[28] the Court had held that a violation of the confrontation req-

uisite was "a constitutional error of the first magnitude and no amount
of showing of want of prejudice would cure it."[29] One writer in the
1983 edition of the *Journal of Criminal Law and Criminology* opined
that "the harmless error standards as currently applied in review of
criminal trials are eroding the integrity of the criminal justice system."[30]

1.3 HISTORICAL BACKGROUND OF THE
SPEEDY TRIAL

The U.S. Supreme Court in Barker v. Wingo[31] traced the origins of
speedy trial to the English Assize of Clarendon in 1166,[32] and to the
Magna Carta of 1215,[33] and further observed that in the first colonial
bill of rights, the Virginia Declaration of Rights of 1776,[34] the right
to a speedy trial was set forth. Nine of the earliest states had similar
provisions in their constitutions.[35] Today it would appear that every
state constitution guarantees its citizens the right to a speedy trial.[36]

Senior Judge Irving R. Kaufman of the Second U.S. Court of Appeals on October 16, 1987, spelled out his views on "the public's
right to speedier justice" in the *New York Times*.[37] He pointed out that
the "most pressing" problems are "the twin demons of expense and
delay":

Ten years ago the median time for filing suit to the commencement of trial in
the Federal district court was less than a year; today it exceeds a year and a
half. Simple cases commonly take more than five years from commencement
to final disposition, and complex litigation . . . can linger more than a de-
cade. . . . Moreover, the longer a suit continues, the more its costs mount.[38]

Thus, the pragmatics of the scenario are simply that the constitutional rights of speedy and fair criminal trials must surmount the com-
plexities of delay and costs.

NOTES

1. 456 US 1 (1982).
2. See United States v. Marion, 404 US 307 (1971).
3. See Section 8.1 of chapter 8 herein.
4. See Section 4.2 of chapter 4 herein.

5. 18 USC 3161-3174 (1982).
6. 18 USC App 545 (1982).
7. See Section 48(b) of Fed R Crim P (1982).
8. See generally 74 Georgetown L J 685 (1986).
9. See Section 3.1 of chapter 3 herein.
10. 398 US 37 (1970).
11. Infra note 9. See Duncan v. Louisiana, 391 US 145 (1968) at 148, Klopfer v. North Carolina, 386 US 213 (1967).
12. _____AD²ᵈ _____, _____NYS²ᵈ _____ (app Div 2, May 23, 1988).
13. See McNabb v. United States, 318 US 332 (1943) at 340.
14. See Barron v. Mayor of Baltimore, 7 Pet (US) 243 (1833).
15. Note Justice Frankfurter's concurring opinion in Francis v. Resweber, 329 US 459 (1947) at 468.
16. See Snyder v. Massachusetts, 291 US 97 (1934) at 105.
17. See generally 100 Harv L Rev 100 (1986) at 107 et seq.
18. 28 USC 2111 (1982).
19. 386 US 18 (1967) at 22.
20. See generally 53 Minn L Rev 519 (1969).
21. See Section 7.1 of chapter 7 herein.
22. See chapter 10 herein.
23. Id.
24. Infra note 19 at 23.
25. 106 S Ct 1431 (1986).
26. 106 S Ct 3101 (1986).
27. Infra note 17 at 108.
28. 415 US 308 (1973).
29. Id. at 318.
30. See 74 J Crim L & Crimin 457 (1983) at 470.
31. 407 US 514 (1972).
32. See 2 Eng Histor Doc 408 (1953). Also see Case & Comment (July–August 1986) at 12.
33. See Coke, The Second Part of the Institutes of the Laws of England 45 (Brooke, 5th ed., 1797).
34. See Va Decl of Rights (1776) at §8.
35. Note Del. Const, 1972, Art. 1, §7; MD Declaration of Rights, 1776, Art. XIX; Pa Declaration of Rights, 1776, §8 Mass. Const., 1780, Part 1, Art. XI; New Hampshire Const., 1784, Part 1, Art. XIV. See also Vermont Const. 1786. c 1. Art. XIV; Ky. Const. 1792, Art. XII, §10; Tenn. Const. 179, Art. XI, §9.
36. See Klopfer v. North Carolina, infra note 11.
37. At A38.
38. Id.

2

The Fair and Speedy Criminal Trial Under the Sixth Amendment

2.1 INTRODUCTION

The Sixth Amendment to the U.S. Constitution reads as follows:

In all criminal prosecutions, the accused shall enjoy the right to a speedy and public trial, by an impartial jury of the State and district wherein the crime shall have been committed, which district shall have been previously ascertained by law, and to be informed of the nature and cause of the accusation; to be confronted with witnesses against him; to have compulsory process for obtaining witnesses in his favor, and to have the Assistance of Counsel for his defense.

2.2 THE RIGHT OF CONFRONTATION

In the words of the Sixth Amendment, "to be confronted with the witnesses against him," is the essence of this right of confrontation, designed to promote reliability in the truth-seeking process.[1] This confrontational right of the criminal defendant includes the right to cross-examine the witnesses whose accusations are made under oath; the confrontational right takes place in front of the jury so that the demeanor of the witnesses can be judged.[2] In Lee v. Illinois[3] the U.S. Supreme Court in 1986 proclaimed that "no one would deny the value of cross-examination in exposing falsehood and bringing out the truth in a criminal case." Earlier the highest court in SEC v. Jerry T. O'Brien, Inc.[4] had held that the confrontation clause was not violated when a federal administrative agency used its subpoena power to gather evidence against an individual without notifying the individual under investigation; the Court reasoned that the confrontation clause cannot be violated until the initiation of criminal proceedings. Under Section 11 (c)(3) of the Federal Rules of Criminal Procedure federal courts cannot accept a plea of guilty or nolo contendere without first informing the defendant of his right to confront and cross-examine witnesses.

The accused defendant exercises the right of confrontation primarily by cross-examination of witnesses. But there is no right of confrontation of persons who are not witnesses.[5] However, the Ninth U.S. Court of Appeals ruled that the trial court's refusal to grant the defendant's request that the participating prosecutor be recused to enable defendant to call the prosecutor as a witness was error and violated defendant's Sixth Amendment rights.[6] A prosecutor, however, has no obligation to call all or certain witnesses against the defendant; in United States v. Howard[7] it was held that defendant's right of confrontation was not violated when defendant's counsel declined to cross-examine certain witnesses. This right to cross-examine encompasses the essential issues of guilt or innocence of the defendant and the credibility of the witness or witnesses against the defendant. Of course, the court may limit cross-examination where the questions are deemed prejudicial,[8] irrelevant,[9] or likely to confuse the jury.[10] But the trial court may not exclude evidence on the basis of the defendant's failure to comply with certain procedural statutes or rules,[11] for by such judicial conduct the defendant's Sixth Amendment rights would be violated. In Stevens v. Bordenkircher[12] the Sixth U.S. Court of Appeals found that the trial court's failure to permit cross-examination of a key government witness about his bias, prejudice, or motive precluded the jury from making a discriminating appraisal of the witness, to the detriment of the defendant's right of confrontation. But on January 25, 1988, in Taylor v. Illinois[13] the U.S. Supreme Court ruled, in a 5–3 decision, that criminal trial judges may bar defense witnesses from testifying in order to punish attorneys for failing to disclose the witnesses' identities soon enough; trial courts were empowered to take the action regardless of the fact that the defendant was not at fault. Here Taylor was convicted on a charge of attempted murder for shooting Bridges in a street fight involving several people. While prosecution witnesses testified that they saw Taylor shoot Bridges, two friends of Taylor testified as defense witnesses that Bridges' brother mistakingly shot Bridges while trying to protect Bridges. On the second day of trial Taylor's attorney sought to add another witness who would have testified that the Bridges' brothers had the guns before the incident, but Taylor's attorney violated a state law by failing to include this witness on the list of witnesses he filed in response to a routine pre-trial request by the prosecution. The trial judge ruled that the violation was deliberate and the proposed testimony so suspect that it was inadmissible. The highest Court's majority opinion pointed out that the defendant's constitutional rights to a fair trial and to call witnesses in his behalf had not been violated. The Court sensed that Taylor's attorney was seeking to obtain a tactical advantage, and perhaps to present fabricated testimony, by denying the prosecution the opportunity to obtain evidence casting doubt on the credibility of the proposed witness. But the dissenting opinions responded that "there was no evidence that the defendant (himself) played any role" in his attorney's violation of the state witness-disclosure rule. The dissent also proclaimed that "an innocent man may be serving 10 years in prison" because of a state trial judge's decision to bar a witness from giving testimony in support of the defense: "A sanction that itself distorts the truth-seeking process by excluding material evidence of innocence in a criminal case" violates the Sixth Amendment right of the defendant to compel testimony of witnesses for his defense. And the dissent concluded: "Deities may be able to visit the sins of the father on the son, but I cannot agree that courts should be able to visit the sins of the lawyer on the innocent client."

The hearsay rule is also designed to protect the criminal defendant, but one type of statement excluded from the heresay rule under Section 801(d)(2)(E) of the Federal Rules of Evidence, for example, is "a statement by a co-conspirator of a party during the course and in furtherance of the conspiracy." In Glasser v. United States[14] the U.S. Supreme Court recognized the potential for unfairness arising from the introduction of alleged statements by a co-conspirator against the defendant. Here the same attorney represented both co-conspirators, and the highest court ruled that the appointment of counsel per se compromised defendant's defense; but co-conspirator statements to third persons "are admissible over the objection of an alleged co-conspirator who was not only present when the statement was made, only if there is some proof aliunde that he is connected with the inquiry. Otherwise, hearsay would lift itself by its own bootstraps to the level of competent evidence."[15] In Bourjaily v. United States[16] in 1987 the highest court rejected the defendant's proposition that out-of-court statements by a co-conspirator are unreliable and therefore inadmissible until the conspiracy is shown: "each one of Lonardo's statements may itself be unreliable, but taken as a whole, the entire conversation between Lonardo and the informant was corroborated by independent evidence." Thus, the defendant's right of confrontation was not infringed upon by the admission of the allegedly untested and possibly unreliable evidence. But it is submitted that the highest court actually eroded the protection of the right of confrontation by holding that particularized indicia of reliability need not be ascertained to satisfy the Sixth Amendment. The admission of hearsay evidence against a defendant violates the Sixth Amendment because it prevents the accused defendant from confronting the out-of-court declarant.[17] And in Bruton v. United States[18] the court had held in 1968 that the admission in a joint trial of hearsay evidence, to wit: the co-defendant's extrajudicial confession incriminating the defendant, had violated the criminal defendant's right of confrontation when the co-defendant did not testify at trial.[19]

In Cruz v. New York[20] in a 5–4 decision the highest court reaffirmed Bruton v. United States[21] and Lee v. Illinois[22] by excluding a co-defendant's confession that corroborated the defendant's admissible confession. The fact that the defendant's and the co-defendant's confessions interlocked could be prejudicial because the co-defendant's confession could confirm the admissions that the defendant had made but wished to avoid. The decision in 1987 reflected the fear that the jury was likely to disregard instructions about the limited admissibility of the confession. But the highest court in Richardson v. Marsh,[23] also in 1987, refused to extend the Bruton case[24] to cover a co-defendant's confession that had been redacted to omit any reference to the defendant but was linked to him by properly admitted evidence: "An interlocking (confession) bears a positively inverse relationship to devastation." Yet earlier in the 1986 case of United States v. Inadi[25] the highest court had placed strict limitations on the scope of the defendant's confrontation clause rights in conspiracy cases: "Co-conspirator statements derive much of their value from the fact that they are made in a context very different from trial, and therefore are usually irreplaceable as substantive evidence.'' Then in the 1987 case of Pennsylvania v. Ritchie[26] the same court emphasized that the confrontation clause guarantees only an opportunity for cross-examination, ''not cross-examination that is effective in whatever way, and to whatever extent, the defendant might wish.''[27]

Two 1988 court decisions, one by the U.S. Supreme Court, the other by the Indiana Supreme Court, illustrate the continuing mode of confrontation issues. In United States v. Owens[28] the highest court answered the following question in the negative, i.e., will the Sixth Amendment's confrontation clause or the Federal Rules of Evidence[29] bar testimony about a prior, out-of-court identification when the identifying witness is unable—due to memory loss—to explain the basis for the identification? The confrontation clause guarantees only an opportunity for effective cross-examination, and that guarantee is satisfied when the defendant has a full and fair opportunity to bring out the witness's bad memory and other facts that tend to discredit his testimony. However, the two dissenting opinions argued that ''the confrontation clause guarantees more than the right to ask questions of a live witness, no matter how dead that witness's memory proves to be.''

The Indiana decision, Miller v. State of Indiana[30] concerned the admission of a videotaped statement of a molested child who did not testify at the defendant's trial. The court ruled that the constitutional right of confrontation prohibits its admissibility into evidence, unless the criminal defendant has an opportunity for cross-examination.

2.3 THE RIGHT OF THE CRIMINAL DEFENDANT TO BE PRESENT AT HIS/HER TRIAL

The Sixth Amendment in guaranteeing the right of confrontation implicitly guarantees the criminal defendant the right to be present at his/her trial, i.e., at all stages of the trial.[31] In Diaz v. United States[32] the defendant in a felony case was deemed to have the right to attend all stages of the trial from the impaneling of the jury to the delivery of the verdict or judgment. But the defendant's right to be present at trial was not violated where defendant was physically unable to attend an evidentiary suppression hearing at which his defense counsel was present.[33] In People v. Washington[34] the defendant, charged with robbery, failed to return from a recess (after having been warned by the court on several occasions) during a pre-trial hearing prepartory to jury selection, and a mistrial was declared. Defendant's counsel moved to suspend proceedings until the defendant returned, but the New York court ruled that the court would proceed with the trial in absentia,[35] because the defendant had knowingly and voluntarily relinquished his right to be present at his trial. It was absurd for the defendant to believe that his absence voluntarily and knowingly would halt the proceedings, according to the court. As pointed out by the U.S. Supreme Court in Taylor v. United States[36] a defendant's voluntary absence during trial can constitute a waiver of his right to be present. This waiver is valid even where there is no showing that the court had warned him (which was not the case here) that the trial would continue in his absence; and thereby a defendant foreclosed his concomitant right to confront witnesses against him/her and to have them testify on his own behalf. The New York court here traced historically to "the very inception of our jurisprudence, a defendant's appearance in a criminal case" which historically was "non-waivable."[37] But New York favors a more restrictive view, as illustrated by the New York Court of Appeals decision in People v. Parker[38] where that court held that when a criminal defendant has been informed of the date for trial and has nonetheless voluntarily failed to appear, it is not sufficient, as a matter of law, for the trial court to proceed to try the defendant in absentia. The highest New York court reasoned that the constitutional right of an accused to be present at trial is fundamental, and that the validity of any waiver of that right must be tested according to constitutional standards. Such standards would require a showing that the defendant was informed of the nature of the right to be present as well as the consequences of failing to appear for trial, including the fact that the trial will proceed in his absence.[39] A 1985 holding by the New York Court of Appeals in People v. Smith[40] found that court willing to proclaim that the defendant who absconded after the third day of the hearing had forfeited his right to be present at trial; and in People v. Sanchez[41] the same court the same year had opined: "There is no significant difference between the misconduct of a defendant who deliberately leaves the courtroom shortly after the trial begins, and that of a defendant who does so after he has been told that the trial is about to begin. In either case his conduct unambiguously indicates a defiance of the processes of law and it disrupts the trial after all the parties are assembled and ready to proceed."[42]

It is within the discretion of the trial judge to determine whether the trial proceeds in the absence of the criminal defendant. In United States v. Muzevsky[43] the Fourth U.S. Court of Appeals advised the trial court to consider such factors as the difficulty in rescheduling the trial, the possibility of prejudice to the government and co-defendants, the likelihood that the criminal defendant will soon reappear, and the need for preservation of testimony; however, when the trial court knows of no reasons for the defendant's failure to appear for trial and has no reason to believe that the trial could be rescheduled within a reasonable period of time, the difficulty the government will encounter in reassembling its proof, as well as other factors, may require proceeding with the trial "as is."

Disruption of the trial by obstreperous behavior of the defendant justifies the exclusion of the criminal defendant from the courtroom,[44] especially after the trial court has issued a warning. It would appear that binding and gagging a defendant during trial reduces the defendant's ability to communicate with counsel, and is therefore less preferable than outright exclusion of the obstreperous defendant from the trial.[45]

Presence of the defendant at his/her criminal trial was the concern in 1934 of Justice Cardozo (and the U.S. Supreme Court) in Snyder v. Massachusetts,[46] who opined that

nowhere in the decisions of this Court is there a dictum, and still less a ruling, that the Fourteenth Amendment assures the privilege of presence when presence would be useless, or the benefit but a shadow. . . . The Fourteenth Amendment has not said in so many words that he must be present every second or minute or even every hour of the trial. . . . Due process of law requires that the proceedings shall be fair, but fairness is relative, not an absolute concept. It is fairness with reference to particular conditions or particular results.[47]

But the U.S. Supreme Court in its 1987 decision in Kentucky v. Stincer[48] ruled that the confrontation clause was not absolute in protecting the defendant's right to be present at criminal proceedings against him; here the exclusion of the defendant from the competency hearing of two child witnesses against him was held not to violate the confrontation clause nor the due process of law clause. The defendant had been charged with committing first degree sodomy against the two children, and the trial judge had conducted an in-camera hearing to determine whether the children were competent to testify. Exclusion of the defendant was justified because he had a right of cross-examination at trial, and therefore defendant's exclusion from the pre-trial hearing did not contribute to any unfairness of that hearing, which dealt with factual background of the children, not with substantive issues surrounding the defendant.

2.4 THE RIGHT TO A PUBLIC TRIAL

The Sixth Amendment guarantees the criminal defendant the right to a public trial, and this right of a public trial is extended to state prosecutions through the due process clause of the Fourteenth Amendment.[49] The rationale for the public trial is undoubtedly the maintenance of public confidence in the criminal justice system itself as well as the provision of an emotional outlet valve for community reaction to crime; other reasons might encompass assurance that the judges and the prosecutors are properly fulfilling their duties and responsibilities and that responsible witnesses to the crime will come forward and will testify truthfully.[50] A criminal defendant has the option of waiving his/her right to a public trial,[51] but the criminal defendant has no constitutional right to a *private* trial.[52] The U.S. Supreme Court has held that the right of the public and of the press-media to attend criminal trials is implicit in the guarantees of the First Amendment.[53] Interestingly, the Sixth Amendment does not give the defendant any right to videotape his/her criminal trial for later profitable broadcast;[54] nor is the Sixth Amendment violated by Rule 53 of the Federal Rules of Criminal Procedure which bars the taking of photographs in open court.[55] Telecasts of state criminal trials do not violate the due process clause of the Fifth Amendment, nor otherwise infringe upon the fundamental rights of the criminal defendant.[56]

It should be observed that the criminal defendant's right to a public trial actually extends to all proceedings including pre-trial evidence suppression hearings.[57] Closure of the criminal courtroom is frowned upon, although the defendant's right to a fair trial and the privacy rights of prospective jurors have been cited as possible justifications for a closed, non-public criminal trial.[58]

In People v. Colon[59] the New York Court of Appeals in 1988 ob-

served that the defendant was charged with criminal sale and possession of cocaine, and that, after the close of the evidence and prior to
the charge to the jury, the trial judge had stated that "as was his
practice," he intended to close the courtroom so that the jury would
not be distracted by spectators coming and going. No one could leave
and no one could enter the courtroom, and defense counsel objected
on the grounds that sealing of the courtroom violated the defendant's
right to a public trial. But New York's highest court disagreed:

Unlike orders explictly excluding members of the public, the trial court's action here does not explicitly exclude anybody and is designed solely to regulate the ingress and egress of spectators. . . . Locking the doors during the
charge to avoid disruption—allowing those already present to remain—does
not seek to exclude the public or frustrate the salutary purpose of public scrutiny. Here, members of the press or public were permitted to attend the charge
to the jury, upon the condition that they arrive at the beginning of the court's
delivery and not leave until instructions have been completed.

The court also surveyed Anglo-American jurisprudence since the abolition of the Star Chamber in 1641 and concluded that the right to a
public trial is not absolute; there are such bounds as the avoidance of
prejudicial publicity, protection of an undercover agent, and the protection of a child witness, inter alia.[60]

It is interesting to observe that there is a public right to attend meetings of legislative bodies, as illustrated by WJR-TV, Inc. v. Cleve-
land.[61] It is a qualified right, however; but the principle is that "existing case law and good sense compel the conclusion that the First
Amendment mandates that the legislative process be made generally
available to the press and to the public."

2.5 COMPULSORY PROCESS AND THE
CRIMINAL TRIAL

It is clear that the Sixth Amendment preserves the right of the defendant in a criminal trial to have compulsory process for obtaining
favorable witnesses.[62] But this right to compulsory process is not absolute, for it requires a showing that the witnesses' testimony would
be both material and favorable to the defense.[63] This right to compul-

sory process was made applicable to state criminal trials through the Fourteenth Amendment.[64]

A witness's Fifth Amendment right against self-incrimination naturally overrides the criminal defendant's right to compulsory process.[65] The criminal defendant cannot expect a favorable witness to waive his/her self-incrimination privilege; nor must the prosecuting authority grant immunity to the favorable witness just to satisfy the defendant's right to compulsory process.[66]

The right to compulsory process extends to both oral and documentary evidence,[67] and presumes adequate time to secure such witnesses and such testimony.[68] Yet it must be observed that the Sixth Amendment can give the right to compulsory process only to the extent that it is within governmental power to give it; a missing or fleeing witness may not be apprehended in time nor even willing to testify.[69] The right to compulsory process does not mandate the procurement of favorable witnesses at government expense, except for indigent defendants who may secure attendance of material witnesses at government expense upon order of the trial court.[70]

2.6 PROCEDURAL FAIRNESS AT THE CRIMINAL TRIAL

Implicit in the Sixth Amendment guarantees for the criminal defendant is the guarantee of a fair trial, not limited to trial "by an impartial jury," but resplendent with every consistent procedural standard for fairness and equity.[71] Fairness is admittedly a difficult quality to define for it embraces every aspect of the criminal procedure from due process of law to equal treatment before the law, from the basic accusatory procedure to the detailed accusation, from the fair judge to the fair and impartial jury, etc.[72] As voiced in Lisenba v. California[73] the trial itself must observe "that fundamental fairness essential to the very concept of justice."

Certainly the trial must be public,[74] and the criminal defendant must enjoy the right of confrontation,[75] the right to be present at the trial,[76] the right to compulsory process,[77] and the right to a speedy trial.[78] The criminal trial must be more than a mere pretense of a trial[79] such as when there is knowing use by the prosecution of perjured testimony or there is willful withholding of favorable evidence for the defendant or the use of false evidence.[80] A trial held in an atmosphere of mob domination violates the fair trial requisite of the Sixth Amendment.[81]

2.7 THE SPEEDY CRIMINAL TRIAL

The Sixth Amendment states that "in all criminal prosecutions, the accused shall enjoy the right to a speedy . . . trial," and the U.S. Supreme Court in its 1972 decision in Barker v. Wingo[82] established four criteria for analyzing the defendant's right to a speedy trial, to wit: (1) the length of the delay; (2) the reasons for the delay; (3) whether and how the defendant asserted the right to a speedy trial; and (4) the amount of prejudice that the defendant has suffered.[83] Obviously, each case must be considered on an ad hoc basis, and the trial court must exercise its discretion in considering other pertinent and material criteria in ascertaining the speedy trial right of the criminal defendant.

The first factor of "length of the delay" is generally measured from the date of the indictment or the date of the arrest, whichever is earlier.[84] The second criterion of "reasons for the delay" might consider whether a party intended to gain a decided unfair advantage thereby, but the delay itself is generally construed strongly against the government that has the duty to bring the matter to trial speedily.[85] However, in United States v. Loud Hawk[86] the U.S. Supreme Court excused the government's delay since it was due to an interlocutory appeal filed by the government. The third criterion as to "whether and how the defendant asserted" the right to a speedy trial is dependent upon a judicial finding that the defendant acted timely and vigorously to assert his/her right.[87] And the fourth criterion of "the amount of prejudice the defendant has suffered" depends upon the interests to be protected. In United States v. Reale[88] the Second U.S. Court of Appeals on December 1, 1987, ruled that a defendant, whose indictment was dismissed without prejudice because of a violation of the Speedy Trial Act, had no right of appeal because "the right to a speedy trial is meant to protect the defendant from delay, not from the trial itself." Here the defendant who had been indicted for federal extortion had won dismissal of the indictment and sought to have the charges dismissed with prejudice which result would have prevented any possibility of his re-indictment. The federal appellate court opined that the trial court's order did not "conclusively dispose of the issue of prejudice" because

actual prejudice is more readily ascertained after trial. . . . The claim that a violation of defendant's speedy trial rights has adversely affected the fact-finding process is not an independent issue; it is inextricably connected to the merits of the case. . . . Unlike the right not to be placed twice in jeopardy, the speedy trial right is not irretrievably lost if not vindicated before trial. . . . That right can be vindicated by acquittal or by reversal on direct appeal from a final judgment of conviction, if the defendant was indeed aggrieved by the fact that earlier dismissal was without prejudice. . . . By further delaying the trial, allowing a speedy trial exception to the rule requiring finality of judgments as a predicate for appellate jurisdiction would disserve the very interests the Act seeks to protect.[89]

Clearly the right to a speedy trial also precludes oppressive pre-trial incarceration, minimizes anxiety and concern of the criminal defendant, and averts the possibility that delay will impair the defense.[90] The requirement of speedy trial has had some unusual effects, as shown in State of Washington v. Alvin,[91] where there was a delay in filing criminal charges that resulted in the loss of juvenile court jurisdiction for the 17-year old defendant. But the Washington Supreme Court opined that due process of law does not require the State to depart from its normal investigatory and administrative procedures so as to give special treatment to a suspect whose 18th birthday is approaching. If the State cannot reasonably justify the delay or if the prejudice to the defendant is fundamentally unjust, there would be a violation of due process of law.

On the other hand, a federal district court judge in Connecticut in Flowers v. Warden[92] ruled that eighteen months in jail before the State could provide the defendant a trial prompted the release of a defendant charged with murder: "The right to a speedy trial is the right of all citizens, not just the innocent. It is a right which is not lessened in retrospect by a finding of guilt." The crowded calendar "cannot justify the violation of petitioner's constitutional right." In People v. Irons[93] the court stated that the State of New York could not expand its time by pleading the misdemeanor counts that were jurisdictionally defective, but the State was bound by the thirty-day period for bringing defendants to trial. However, in People v. Vrlaku[94] the criminal defendant, while under indictment for assault and while free on bail, fled the jurisdiction and embarked upon a crime spree in Illinois, Texas, and Florida. Federal criminal proceedings in those States caused other delays in securing the defendant's extradition to New York. In New York the defendant moved to dismiss the indictments on the ground that he had not been brought to trial within 180 days as required by the Interstate Agreement on Detainer.[95] The State of New York contended that the speedy trial requirement had been tolled by a tolling provision of the agreement "whenever and for as long as the prisoner is unable to stand trial," and the court agreed.

2.8 SIXTH AMENDMENT RIGHTS IN FEDERAL MAGISTRATE COURTS

As pointed out in the Winter 1986 issue of the *University of San Francisco Law Review*,[96] there are myriads of problems associated with the Sixth Amendment rights for defendants accused of state crimes in federal magistrate courts. An individual accused of a non-petty misdemeanor, i.e., offenses punishable by a term of imprisonment of less than one year,[97] is entitled to the guarantees of the Sixth Amendment. Federal law also provides that a person may be prosecuted for a state crime which is committed on federally owned or federally controlled property where no similar crime exists under federal law.[98] It is up to the respective state to delineate the particular misdemeanor as petty or non-petty, with the result that federal defendants prosecuted for similar non-petty misdemeanors in different states may not be afforded equivalent Sixth Amendment protection.[99] The thrust of the timely law review article[100] is to curb the inadvertent impact of state law on the constitutional rights of defendants charged with state crimes in federal courts.

NOTES

1. See generally 53 Fordham L Rev 1291 (1985).
2. Note Lee v. Illinois, 106 S Ct 2056 (1986) to the effect that "the right of cross-examination is included in the right of an accused in a criminal case to confront the witnesses against him" (at 2062).
3. Infra note 2 at 2062.
4. 467 US 735 (1984).

5. See Davis v. Alaska, 415 US 308 (1974).
6. See United States v. Prantil, 764 F2d 548 (9th Cir., 1985).
7. 751 F2d 336 (10th Cir., 1984).
8. See Haber v. Wainright, 756 F2d 1520 (11th Cir. 1985), and United States v. Bittner, 728 F2d 1038 (8th Cir., 1984).
9. See United States v. Wellington, 754 F2d 1457 (9th Cir., 1985).
10. Note United States v. Balliviero, 708 F2d 934 (5th Cir., 1983).
11. See Ruff v. Wyrick, 709 F2d 1219 (8th Cir., 1983).
12. 746 F2d 342 (6th Cir., 1984).
13. 108 S Ct. 145 (January 25, 1988).
14. 315 US 60 (1942).
15. Id. at 74–75.
16. 107 S Ct 2775 (1987).
17. See Ohio v. Roberts, 448 US 56 (1980) at 63.
18. 391 US 123 (1968).
19. Id. at 126.
20. 107 S Ct 1714 (1987).
21. Infra note 19.
22. Infra note 3.
23. 107 S Ct 1702 (1987).
24. Infra note 19.
25. 475 US 387 (1986).
26. 107 S Ct 989 (1987).
27. Note United States v. Owens, 789 F2d 750 (3rd Cir., 1986), where the confrontation clause was violated when the witness suffered from memory loss and could not be effectively cross-examined about contradictory testimony. See generally ABAJ (January 1, 1988) at 35 et seq.
28. _____US_____, _____SCt_____ (February 15, 1988).
29. _____Rule 801 (d)(1)(C) thereof.
30. _____NE2d_____ (Ind., December 29, 1987).
31. See Illinois v. Allen, 397 US 337 (1970).
32. 223 US 442 (1912).
33. See United States v. Pepe, 747 F2d 632 (11th Cir., 1984).
34. _____NYS2d_____ (Bronx County, November 23, 1987).
35.

The popular mythology is that trial in absentia is a practice utilized by the more repressive regimes of Eastern Europe. The misconception is belied by the fact that such trials, with appropriate safeguards, are a function of American law. . . . As civilization and the law developed, and trial by battle gave way to trial by jury, the right to be present retained its vitality in order to guarantee to the defendant his participation at all crucial parts of his trial, and to prevent the evil of secret trials (People v. Epps, 37 N.Y. 2d 343, 348 [1975]). The common law courts deemed this right a requisite to jurisdiction, absolute and non-waivable (Hopt v. Utah, 110 U.S. 574 [1884]; Ball v. United States,

140 U.S. 118 [1891]; Lewis v. United States, 146 U.S. 370 [1892]). Later cases, however, recognize that while the right exists for the benefit of the accused, where the accused voluntarily chooses to absent himself from the proceedings, it acts as a waiver of the right (Diaz v. United States, 223 U.S. 442 [1912]). Thus, the United States Supreme Court held in Taylor v. United States (414 U.S. 17 [1973] that a defendant's voluntary absence during trial can constitute a waiver of his right to be present. This even where there is no showing that the court had warned him that the trial would continue in his absence; and thereby a defendant forecloses his concomitant right(s) to confront witnesses against him and/or to testify on his own behalf.

36. 414 US 17 (1973).
37.

The reason can be found in the earliest days of Anglo-Saxon legal practice. "When criminal proceedings firsts began to take definite shape . . . [t]he procedure savored of the nature of a civil action in which the community had little or no interest; it was the case of one individual pursuing redress for a private wrong committed by the accused. Obviously, the tribunal, crude as it was, could not entertain a complaint from an aggrieved party unless the presence of the accused was secured" (Goldin, Presence of the Defendant at Rendition of Verdict in Felony Cases, 16 Col. L. Rev. 18 [1916]).

Perhaps an even more compelling reason why the accused's presence was required centered on the methodology determinative of guilt or innocence. "The most common of the early methods transplanted to England was trial by 'ordeal,' and the defendant's presence was necessary in order that he might undergo the ordeal. Later, following the Norman Conquest, the form of trial by 'battle' was developed and continued as the normal method of determining guilt through the days of Glanvill and well into the time of Bracton" (Goldin, supra, at 18). Indeed, trial by battle was provided for in colonial America, and was not formerly abolished in England until 1819 (Kornstein, Richard II—Trial by Combat, N.Y.L.J. 9-29-87, p. 2, c. 3). In trial by battle, as in trial by ordeal, it was, of course, necessary for the accused to be present. "This resulted from the nature of the trial, which was a combat, and every combat presupposed the presence of two combatants, of whom the accused was one" (Goldin, supra, at 19).

38. 57 NY2d 136 (1982).
39. According to the court in the Washington case, infra note 31:

The holdings in Taylor and Parker may be reconciled in that Taylor dealt with a situation in which the defendant absconded after the trial had already commenced whereas in Parker, the defendant had merely been informed of the prospective trial date, and chose not to appear on the day that said trial was scheduled to open, or thereafter. The significance of this fact is that in a situation as existed in Taylor, a defendant's knowledge that the trial would proceed in his absence could be implied, circumstances making it an absurdity for him to believe that the proceedings would be halted where a judge, jury, lawyers and witnesses are present and ready to continue.

40. 66 NY2d 436 (1985).
41. 65 NY2d 436 (1985).

42. Yet the court in the Washington case, infra note 31, had some misgivings:

Even assuming that our courts have determined that a defendant has waived the right to be present, trial in absentia is not thereby automatically authorized. "Rather, the trial court must exercise its sound discretion upon consideration of all appropriate factors, including the possibility that defendant could be located within a reasonable period of time, the difficulty of rescheduling trial and the chance that evidence will be lost or witnesses will disappear" (People v. Parker, 57 N.Y. 2d 136, supra, at 142).

Moreover, if the trial court should decide to proceed against the defendant in absentia, our requirement(s) compels care not to highlight the defendant's absence. Such "highlighting" resulted in reversal in People v. Morales (84 A.D. 2d 522, 1st Dept. [1981]), wherein the trial judge explained to the jury that the defendant was absent for "unexplained and unexcused reasons," permitted the prosecutor in summation to refer to defendant's flight as evidence of a "consciousness of guilt," and charged the jury that they had "the right to infer from these events that the defendant is engaged in flight from prosecution on the charges contained in this indictment" and that such flight could be "interpreted as evidence of consciousness of guilt."

In the case at bar, the Court has afforded a reasonable period of time to locate the defendant, but to no avail. Concern for the case to proceed in a manner preservative of the prosecution's ability to sustain its initial burden combines with a finding that the defendant knowingly, voluntarily and intelligently relinquished his right to be present at trial to deny the defense motion. The case against James Washington is allowed to proceed to trial in absentia.

The above constitutes the decision and order of this Court.

43. 760 F2d 83 (4th Cir., 1985).
44. Infra note 28.
45. Infra note 23 at 334.
46. 291 US 97 (1934).
47.

The underlying principle gains point and precision from the distinction everywhere drawn between proceedings at the trial and those before and after. Many motions before trial are heard in the defendant's absence, and many motions after trial or in the prosecution of appeals. . . . So far as the Fourteenth Amendment is concerned, the presence of a defendant is a condition of due process to the extent that a fair and just hearing would be thwarted by his absence, and to that extent only.

A fertile source of perversion in constitutional theory is the tyranny of labels. Out of the vague precepts of the Fourteenth Amendment a court frames a rule which is general in form, though it has been wrought under the pressure of particular situations. Forthwith another situation is placed under the rule because it is fitted to the words, though related faintly, if at all, to the reasons that brought the rule into existence. A defendant in a criminal case must be present at a trial when evidence is offered, for the opportunity must be his to advise with his counsel . . . and cross-examine his accusers. . . . Let the words "evidence" and "trial" be extended but a little, and the privilege will apply to stages of the cause at which the function of counsel is mechanical or formal and at which a scene and not a witness is to deliver up its message. In such circumstances the solution of the problem is not to be found in dictionary definitions of evidence or trials. It is not to be found in judgments of the courts that at other times or in other circumstances the presence of a defendant is a postulate of justice. There can be no sound solution without answer to the question whether in the particular conditions exhibited by the record the enforced absence of the defendant is so flagrantly unjust that the Constitution of the United States steps in to forbid it. . . . What is here for revision is the action of the judicial department of a state excluding the defendant in a particular set of circumstances, and the justice or injustice of that exclusion must be determined in the light of the whole record. . . . Discretion has not been abdicated. To the contrary, the record makes it clear that discretion has been exercised. . . .

True, indeed, it is that constitutional privileges or immunities may be conferred so explicitly as to leave no room for an inquiry whether prejudice to a defendant has been wrought through their denial. . . . In the same way, privileges, even though not explicit may be so obviously fundamental as to bring us to the same result. A defendant who has been denied an opportunity to be heard in his defense has lost something indispensable, however convincing the *ex parte* showing. But here, in the case at hand, the privilege, if it exists, is not explicitly conferred, nor has the defendant been denied an opportunity to answer and defend.

48. 107 S Ct 2658 (1987).

49. See In Re Oliver, 333 US 257 (1948), and Rovinsky v. McKaskle, 722 F2d 197 (5th Cir., 1984).

50. See generally Press-Enterprise Co. v. Superior Court, 464 US 501 (1984).

51. See Singer v. United States, 380 US 24 (1965).

52. Id. at 35.

53. See Richmond Newspapers, Inc. v. Virginia, 448 US 555 (1980). Note Warren Freedman, "News Media Coverage of Criminal Cases and the Right to a Fair Trial," 40 Nebr L Rev 391 (1961), and Warren Freedman, *Press and Media Access to the Criminal Courtroom* (Quorum, 1988).

54. See United States v. Kerlye, 753 F2d 617 (7th Cir., 1985).

55. Id. at 620.

56. See Chandler v. State of Florida, 449 US 560 (1981).

57. See Waller v. Georgia, 467 US 39 (1984).

58. Infra note 47.

59. _____NY2d_____, _____NE2d_____ (March 22, 1988).

60. Note that the New York Constitution does not contain a guarantee of a public trial; that guarantee is found in the Sixth Amendment to the U.S. Constitution! The New York court concluded:

The right to a public trial has always been recognized as subject to the inherent power of trial courts to administer the activities of the courtroom; suitably within the trial court's discretion is the power to monitor admittance to the courtroom, as the circumstances require, in order to prevent overcrowding, to accommodate limited seating capacity, to maintain sanitary or health conditions, and generally to preserve order and decorum in the courtroom (*People v. Glover*, 60 NY2d 783; *People v. Jelke*, 308 NY 56, 63, *supra*; *People v. Miller*, 257 NY 54, 60).

61. ____F Supp____ (Ohio, March 30, 1988).
62. See Section 2.1 herein.
63. See United States v. Wilson, 732 F2d 404 (5th Cir., 1984) at 412.
64. See Washington v. Texas, 388 US 14 (1967) at 19.
65. See United States v. Thornton, 733 F2d 121 (DC Cir., 1984).
66. Note United States v. Chitty, 760 F2d 425 (2nd Cir., 1985).
67. See United States v. Schneiderman, 106 F Supp 731 (SD Cal., 1952) at 735.
68. See MacKenna v. Ellis, 280 F2d 592 (5th Cir., 1960) at 603.
69. Note United States v. Greco, 298 F2d 247 (2nd Cir., 1962), cert den 369 US 820 (1962); also note United States v. DiGregorio, 148 F Supp 526 (SDNY, 1957).
70. See Fegeur v. United States, 302 F2d 214 (8th Cir., 1962), cert den 371 US 872 (1962).
71. See Irvin v. Dowd, 366 US 717 (1961) at 722.
72. See In Re Murchison, 349 US 133 (1955).
73. 314 US 219 (1941) at 236.
74. See Section 2.4 herein.
75. See Section 2.1 herein.
76. See Section 2.3 herein.
77. See Section 2.5 herein.
78. See Section 2.7 herein.
79. See Mooney v. Holohan, 294 US 103 (1935) at 112.
80. See Brady v. Maryland, 373 US 83 (1963), and People v. Leyra, 302 NY 353 (1951).
81. Note Kasey v. Goodwyn, 291 F2d 174 (4th Cir., 1961), cert den 368 US 959 (1962).
82. 407 US 514 (1972).
83. Id. at 530.
84. See Cain v. Smith, 686 F2d 374 (6th Cir., 1982).
85. See Payne v. Rees, 738 F2d 118 (6th Cir., 1984) at 122.
86. ____US____ (1986).
87. Cf. Look v. Amaral, 725 F2d 4 (1st Cir., 1984).
88. ____F2d____ (2nd Cir., December 1, 1987).
89. 18 USC 3161 to 3174 (1982).
90. See NYLJ (December 8, 1987) at 5.
91. ____P2d____ (Wash., December 10, 1987).
92. ____F Supp____ (Conn., January 22, 1988).
93. ____NYS2d____ (NYLJ, March 15, 1988, at 17, col 4).

94. _____NYS2d_____ (App Div 2nd, January 11, 1988).
95. Section 580.20 of CPL & R.
96. 20 U of San Francisco L Rev 313 (Winter 1986).
97. 18 USC 1(2) (1982). The "petty misdemeanors" are offenses punishable by a term of imprisonment not to exceed 6 months and/or a fine of less than $500; see 18 USC 1 (3) (1982).
98. Section 13 of Title 18 of U.S. Code (1982).
99. See Scott v. Illinois, 440 US 367 (1979).
100. Infra note 96.

3

The Fourteenth Amendment and the Right to a Speedy and a Fair Criminal Trial

3.1 INTRODUCTION

The Fourteenth Amendment, Section 1, inter alia, proclaims that "No State shall make or enforce any law which shall abridge the privileges and immunities of citizens of the United States; nor shall any State deprive any person of life, liberty or property without due process of law; nor deny to any person within its jurisdiction the equal protection of the laws. . . . " Thus, the Fourteenth Amendment placed general restraints upon the states similar to those restraints which the Bill of Rights or the various amendments to the U.S. Constitution placed upon the federal government. In essence, the federal courts became responsible for the caliber of justice in the state courts; yet the U.S. Supreme Court had, in the leading cases of Hurtado v. California[1] and Twining v. New Jersey,[2] it may be argued, rejected the view that the Fourteenth Amendment absorbed the Bill of Rights, and placed upon the states the exact limitations that the various amendments had placed upon the federal government. But the due process clause of the Fourteenth Amendment does express a demand for standards of fair procedure not defined by the specific guarantees of the Bill of Rights.[3] The equal protection clause of the Fourteenth Amendment is "equally" effective with respect to standards not defined by the specific guarantees of the Bill of Rights.

It must be clear that personal rights prevail over property rights, as viewed by the U.S. Supreme Court in its 1938 opinion in United States v. Carolene Products Co.[4] Yet the U.S. Constitution itself established no hierarchy of rights.[5]

In keeping with the spirit of the right to a speedy trial the New York court in People v. Gaston[6] observed that the State has a continuing obligation to maintain its readiness for trial, and that a statement of current readiness at one point does not terminate the continuing obligation.[7] The court found that the total lack of diligence by the State required dismissal of defendant's indictment since under the circumstances the time during which a bench warrant was not enforced by the State was chargeable to the State.

3.2 EQUAL PROTECTION OF THE LAWS

"It seems reasonably clear that the due process of law provision of the Fifth Amendment is broad enough in its scope and purpose to include the Equal Protection of the Laws which no State may deny to any person under the provisions of the Fourteenth Amendment.[8] In the Hurtado case[9] the U.S. Supreme Court opined that "the equal protection clause is associated in the amendment with the due process clause and it is customary to consider them together. It may be that they overlap, that a violation of one may involve at times the violation of the other, but the sphere of the protection they offer are not coterminus." Indeed, our whole system of law is predicated on the general fundamental principal of equality of application of the law: "all men are equal before the law," "this is government of laws and not of men," and "no man is above the law" are all maxims showing the spirit in which the courts are expected to apply the laws. Equality of treatment of all persons, even though they all enjoyed the protection of due process of law, is the summum bonum.[10] Chief Justice Taft in Truax v. Corrigan[11] summarized:

Thus the guaranty was intended to secure equality of protection not only for all but against all similarly situated. Indeed, protection is not protection unless it does so. Immunity granted to a class, however limited, having the effect to deprive another class, however limited, of a personal or property right, is just as clearly a denial of equal protection of the laws to the latter class as if the immunity were in favor of, or the deprivation of right permitted, worked against, a larger class.

Justice Stevens in City of Cleburne v. Cleburne Living Center[12] in 1985 opined: "In every equal protection case we have to ask certain basic questions. What class is harmed by the legislation, and has it been subjected to a 'tradition of disfavor' by our laws? What is the public purpose that is being served by the law? What is the characteristic of the disadvantaged class that justified disparate treatment?"[13]

It would appear that prior to 1976 the U.S. Supreme Court analyzed the equal protection clause in terms of "minimum rationality" for ordinary economic and social problems[14] and in terms of "strict scrutiny" for problems involving fundamental personal rights,[15] application of the latter standard invariably resulting in invalidation of a statute.[16] In 1976 in Craig v. Boren[17] the highest court introduced a third standard of scrutiny, to wit: relationship to an important governmental objective. In Wygant v. Jackson Board of Education[18] the Court invalidated a collective bargaining agreement that, when layoffs became necessary, replaced a strict seniority system with one designed to maintain the then-current percentage of minority teachers. The dissent of Justice Stevens upheld the agreement because he found a relationship to an important governmental interest, to wit: the value of "educating children for the future."[19]

Historically, the equal protection of the laws clause in the Fourteenth Amendment has been litigated vociferously over the years. This is so because of the very nature of the clause. In 1880 in Strauder v. West Virginia,[20] for example, the U.S. Supreme Court pointed out that "the Fourteenth Amendment makes no attempt to enumerate rights it designed to protect. It speaks in general terms, and those are as comprehensive as possible. Its language is prohibitory; but every prohibition implies the existence of rights and immunities, prominent among which is an immunity from inequality of legal protection, either for life, liberty, or property."[21] Thirty-seven years later in Buchanan v. Warley[22] the court proclaimed that any attempt to prevent the alienation of property to a person of color was not a "legitimate exercise of the police power of the State and is in direct violation of the fundamental law enacted in the Fourteenth Amendment of the Constitution preventing State interference. . . ."[23] In 1938 the highest court in Missouri ex rel Gaines v. Canada[24] emphasized that "equal protection of the laws is 'a pledge of the protection of equal laws.' Manifestly, the obligation of the State to give the protection of equal laws can be performed only where its laws operate, that is, within its own jurisdiction. It is there that the equality of legal right must be maintained."[25]

3.3 DUE PROCESS OF LAW

The due process of law clause of the Fourteenth Amendment (and of the Fifth Amendment) was rooted in the Magna Carta of 1215 and was included in the early state constitutions before becoming an integral part of the U.S. Constitution as a limitation upon the executive, legislative, and judicial powers of the federal government and subsequently a limitation on the same powers of the states. The due process clause requires that every person shall have the protection of his/her day in court and the benefit of the general law, a law which hears before it condemns, which proceeds not arbitrarily or capriciously but upon inquiry, and renders judgment only after trial, so that every citizen shall hold his life, liberty, property and immunities under the protection of the general rules which govern society.[26] Due process of law embraces substantive as well as procedural limitations.[27] But the due process clause in the U.S. Constitution "contains no description of those processes which it was intended to allow or forbid. It does not even declare what principles are to be applied to ascertain whether it be due process. It is manifest that it was not left to the legislative power to enact any process which might be devised.[28] In Ownbey v. Morgan[29] the U.S. Supreme Court delineated the essentials of the due process clause, i.e., "the right to appear and be heard in defense of the action," in face of a Delaware statute that conditioned the hearing upon "giving security to the value of the property attached." The Court, however, concluded that "the statutes under consideration were not in conflict with the due process provision of the Fourteenth Amendment." Furthermore, "the due process clause does not impose upon the States a duty to establish ideal systems for the administration of justice with every modern improvement and with provision against every possible hardship that may befall. It restrains State action, whether legislative, executive or judicial, within bounds that are consistent with the fundamentals of individual liberty and private property, including the right to be heard where liberty or property is at stake in judicial proceedings."[30] Years later in Powell v. Alabama[31] the defendants contended that they were "denied due process of law in Alabama in that they were not given a fair, impartial, and deliberate trial; they were denied the right of counsel, with the accustomed incidents of consultation and opportunity of preparation for trial; and they were tried before juries from which qualified members of their own race were systematically excluded." The U.S. Supreme Court agreed, reversed the convictions, and opined that "it was the duty of the court having their cases in charge to see that they were denied no necessary incident of a fair trial.[32]

A criminal statute that fails to provide adequate notice to a person of ordinary intelligence that his contemplated conduct is prohibited offends the due process clause of the Fourteenth Amendment.[33] In short, such an invalidated statute holds one criminally responsible for activity which he could not reasonably understand to be unlawful. This precept of "void for vagueness" not only requires notions of fair notice but also requires legislatures to set reasonably clear guidelines for law enforcement officials and triers of fact in order to prevent arbitrary and discriminatory enforcement. In Elfbrandt v. Russell[34] the highest court in 1966 struck down Arizona legislation designed to ascertain the fitness and competence of all state employees; Justice Douglas stressed that the challenged scheme was not restricted to those who "subscribe to the organization's unlawful ends" or "who join with the specific intent to further illegal action." Justice Cardozo earlier in Palko v. Connecticut[35] had opined that "social and moral values" had been brought within the Fourteenth Amendment "by a process of absorption. These in their origin were effective against the federal government alone. If the Fourteenth Amendment has absorbed them, the process of absorption has had its course in the belief that neither liberty nor justice would exist if they were sacrificed.[36]

In Rochin v. California[37] the highest court in an opinion by Justice Frankfurter found that deputy sheriffs from Los Angeles had violated Fourteenth Amendment due process:

The proceedings by which this conviction had been obtained do more than offend some fastidious squeamishness or private sentimentalism about combatting crime too energetically. This is conduct that shocks the conscience. Illegally breaking into the privacy of the petitioner, the struggle to open his mouth and remove what was there, the forcible extraction of his stomach's contents—this course of proceeding by agents of government to obtain evidence is bound to offend even hardened sensibilities. They are methods too close to the racks and the screw to permit of constitutional differentiation. It has long since ceased to be true that due process of law is heedless of the means by which otherwise relevant and credible evidence is obtained.[38]

The Fifth Amendment provides that

no person shall be held to answer for a capital, or otherwise infamous crime, unless on a presentment or indictment of a Grand Jury, except in cases arising in the land or naval forces, or in the Militia, when in actual service in time of War or public danger; nor shall any person be subject for the same offense to be twice put in jeopardy of life or limb; nor shall be compelled in any criminal case to be a witness against himself, nor be deprived of life, liberty, or property, without due process of law. . . .

It is thus evident that the fair trial is a goal of the Fifth Amendment, at least with respect to self-incrimination and deprivation of life, liberty, or property, without due process of law. Again, the Fourteenth Amendment makes these constitutional guarantees effective against the states.

NOTES

1. 110 US 516 (1884).
2. 211 US 78 (1908).
3. Cf. Justice Frankfurter's concurring opinion in Francis v. Resweber, 329 US 459 (1947) at 468.
4. 304 US 144 (1938) at 152.
5. See the dissent of Justice Jackson in Brinegar v. United States, 338 US 160 (1949) at 180.
6. _____NYS2d_____ (NY County, March 22, 1988).
7. Note People v. Anderson. 66 NY2d 529 (1985).
8. United States v. Yount, 267 Fed 861 (WD. Pa., 1920) at 863.
9. Infra note 1.
10. See Barbier v. Connolly, 113 US 27 (1885) at 32.
11. 257 US 312 (1921) at 331. Note the comments of Justice Van Devanter in Lindsley v. Natural Carbonic Gas Co., 220 US 61 (1911) at 78–79:

The equal protection clause of the Fourteenth Amendment does not take from the State the power to classify in the adoption of police laws, but admits of the exercise of a wide scope of discretion in that regard, and avoids what is done only when it is without any reasonable basis and therefore is purely arbitrary. 2. A classification having some reasonable basis does not offend against that clause merely because it is not made with mathematical nicety or because in practice it results in some inequality. 3. When the classification in such a law is called in question, if any state of facts reasonably can be conceived that would sustain it, the existence of that state of facts at the time the law was enacted must be assumed. 4. One who assails the classification in such a law must carry the burden of showing that it does not rest upon any reasonable basis, but it essentially arbitrary.

12. 105 S Ct 3249 (1985).

13. Id. at 3261-3262. Also see 100 Harv L Rev 1146 (1987) at 1146.

14. See Schweiker v. Wilson, 450 US 221 (1981), and Bowen v. Owens, 106 S Ct 1881 (1986).

15. See Cabell v. Chavez-Salido, 454 US 432 (1982), and Skinner v. Oklahoma, 316 US 535 (1942).

16. See, for example, Local 28, Sheet Metal Workers International Assn. v. EEOC, 106 S Ct 3019 (1986) at 3053.

17. 429 US 190 (1976).

18. 106 S Ct 1842 (1986).

19. Id. at 1867.

20. 100 US 303 (1880).

21. The Court continued:

Any State action that denies this immunity to a colored man is in conflict with the Constitution.

Concluding, therefore, that the statute of West Virginia, discriminating in the selection of jurors, as it does, against negroes because of their color, amounts to a denial of the equal protection of the laws to a colored man when he is put upon trial for an alleged offence against the State, it remains only to be considered whether the power of Congress to enforce the provisions of the Fourteenth Amendment by appropriate legislation is sufficient to justify the enactment of section 641 of the Revised Statutes. . . .

There was error, therefore, in proceeding to the trial of the indictment against him after his petition was filed, as also in overruling his challenge to the array of the jury, and in refusing to quash the panel.

The judgment of the Supreme Court of West Virginia will be reversed, and the case remitted with instructions to reverse the judgment of the Circuit Court of Ohio County; and it is

So ordered.

22. 245 US 60 (1917).

23.

The concrete question here is: May the occupancy, and, necessarily, the purchase and sale of property of which occupancy is an incident, be inhibited by the States, or by one of its municipalities, solely because of the color of the proposed occupant of the premises? That one may dispose of his property, subject only to the control of lawful enactments curtailing that right in the public interest, must be conceded. The question now presented makes it pertinent to inquire into the constitutional right of the white man to sell his property to a colored man, having in view the legal status of the purchaser and occupant. . . .

In the face of these constitutional and statutory provisions, can a white man be denied, consistently with due process of law, the right to dispose of his property to a purchaser by prohibiting the occupation of it for the sole reason tht the purchaser is a person of color intending to occupy the premises as a place of residence? . . . In view of the rights secured by the Fourteenth Amendment to the federal Constitution such legislation must have its limitations, and cannot be sustained where the exercise of authority exceeds the restraints of the Constitution. We think these limitations are exceeded in laws and ordinances of the character now before us.

24. 305 US 337 (1938).

25. The court continued:

That obligation is imposed by the Constitution upon the States severally as governmental entities,—each responsible for its own laws establishing the rights and duties of persons within its borders. It is an obligation the burden of which cannot be cast by one State upon another, and no State can be excused from performance by what another State may do or fail to do. That separate responsibility of each State within its own sphere is of the essence of statehood maintained under our dual system. It seems to be implicit in respondents' argument that if other States did not provide courses for legal education, it would nevertheless be the constitutional duty of Missouri when it supplied such courses for white students to make equivalent provision for negroes. But that plain duty would exist because it rested upon the State independently of the action of other States. We find it impossible to conclude that what otherwise would be unconstitutional discrimination, with respect to the legal right to the enjoyment of opportunities within the State, can be justified by requiring resort to opportunities elsewhere.

26. See Hurtado v. California, 110 US 516 (1884).

27. See generally 42 Yale L J 333 (1933).

28. See Murray's Lessee v. Hoboken Land & Improvement Co., 18 How (US) 272 (1956). The Court continued:

The article is a restraint on the legislative as well as on the executive and judicial powers of the government, and cannot be so construed as to leave Congress free to make any process "due process of law," by its mere will. To what principles, then, are we to resort to ascertain whether this process, enacted by Congress, is due process? To this the answer must be twofold. We must examine the Constitution itself, to see whether this process be in conflict with any of its provisions. If not found to be so, we must look to those settled usages and modes of proceeding existing in the common and statute law of England, before the emigration of our ancestors, and which are shown not to have been unsuited to their civil and political condition by having been acted on by them after the settlement of this country. [T]hough "due process of law" generally implies and includes actor, reus, judex, regular allegations, opportunity to answer, and a trial according to some settled course of judicial proceedings, . . . yet, this is not universally true. There may be, and we have seen that there are cases, under the law of England after Magna Carta, and as it was brought to this country and acted on here, in which process, in its nature final, issues against the body, lands, and goods of certain public debtors without any such trial; . . .

29. 256 US 94 (1921).

30. The Court continued:

However desirable it is that the old forms of procedure be improved with the progress of time, it cannot rightly be said that the Fourteenth Amendment furnishes a universal and self-executing remedy. Its function is negative, not affirmative, and it carries no mandate for particular measures of reform. For instance, it does not constrain the States to accept particular modern doctrines of equity, or adopt a combined system of law and equity procedure, or dispense with all necessity for form and method in pleading, or give untrammeled liberty to make amendments. Neither does it, as we think, require a State to relieve the hardship of an ancient and familiar method of procedure by dispensing with the exaction of special security from an appearing defendant in foreign attachment.

31. 287 US 45 (1932).

32. The Court found denial of the right of counsel infringing the due process clause:

One test which has been applied to determine whether due process of law has been accorded in given instances is to ascertain what were the settled usages and modes of proceeding under the common and statute law of England before the Declaration of Independence, subject, however, to the qualification that they be shown not to have been unsuited to the civil and political conditions of our ancestors by having been followed in this country after it became a nation. . . . Plainly, as appears from the foregoing, this test, as thus qualified, has not been met in the present case. . . .

In the light of the facts outlined in the forepart of this opinion—the ignorance and illiteracy of the defendants, their youth, the circumstances of public hostility, the imprisonment and the close surveillance of the defendants by the military forces, the fact that their friends and families were all in other states and communication with them necessarily difficult, and above all that they stood in deadly peril of their lives—we think the failure of the trial court to give them reasonable time and opportunity to secure counsel was a clear denial of due process.

But passing that, and assuming their inability, even if opportunity had been given, to employ counsel, as the trial court evidently did assume, we are of opinion that, under the circumstances just stated, the necessity of counsel was so vital and imperative that the failure of the trial court to make an effective appointment of counsel was likewise a denial of due process within the meaning of the Fourteenth Amendment. . . .

33. See, for example, Papachristou v. City of Jacksonville, 405 US 156 (1972).

34. 384 US 11 (1966).

35. 302 US 319 (1937).

36. The highest court continued: "This is true, for illustration, of freedom of thought and speech. Of that freedom one may say that it is the matrix, the indispensable condition, of nearly every other form of freedom. . . . Fundamental too in the concept of due process, and so in that of liberty, is the

thought that condemnation shall be rendered only after trial. The hearing, moreover, must be a real one, not a sham or pretense. . . . "

37. 342 US 165 (1952).

38. The Court continued:

Due process of law, as a historic and generative principle, precludes defining, and thereby confining, these standards of conduct more precisely than to say that convictions cannot be brought by methods that offend "a sense of justice." It would be a stultification of the responsibility which the course of constitutional history has cast upon this Court to hold that in order to convict a man the police cannot extract by force what is in his mind but can extract what is in his stomach.

To attempt in this case to distinguish what lawyers call "real evidence" from verbal evidence is to ignore the reasons for excluding coerced confessions. Use of involuntary verbal confessions in State criminal trials is constitutionally obnoxious not only because of their unreliability. They are inadmissible under the Due Process Clause even though statements contained in them may be independently established as true. Coerced confessions offend the community's sense of fair play and decency. So here, to sanction the brutal conduct which naturally enough was condemned by the court whose judgment is before us, would be to afford brutalilty the cloak of law. Nothing would be more calculated to discredit law and thereby to brutalize the temper of a society.

4

Time Criteria for the Speedy Criminal Trial Under the Sixth Amendment

4.1 INTRODUCTION

The defendant's right to a speedy criminal trial has constitutional underpinnings other than the Sixth Amendment's express speedy trial procedure.[1] The due process clause of the Fifth Amendment, for example, protects the criminal defendant against intentional and prejudicial pre-accusation delay.[2] Statutory underpinnings of the criminal defendant's right to a speedy trial include the Interstate Agreement on Detainers Act of 1970,[3] the Federal Rules of Criminal Procedure,[4] and the Speedy Trial Act of 1974[5] which established specific time limits to ensure that the various stages of a criminal proceeding progress according to proper measure.[6] State statutes like New York's CPL also set statutory time limits; in People v. Spadafora[7] the New York Appellate Division, First Dept., in 1987 ruled that a delay in the government's readiness for trial can be excluded from the statutory time limits under the exception only

if during the crucial time period the prosecutor exercised due diligence to obtain the unavailable evidence and reasonable ground existed to believe that such evidence would become available in a reasonable period of time. Due diligence alone will not suffice. Since at no time during the 7-month period preceding the making of defendant's speedy trial motion did a reasonable basis exist to believe that Jon would become available, the People's claim to the benefit of this statutory exception must fail.[8]

The U.S. Supreme Court in 1966 in State of North Carolina v. Klopfer[9] had ruled that the right to speedy criminal trial to be as fundamental as "any of the rights secured by the Sixth Amendment." Here, in a misdemeanor charge of criminal trespass against a university professor, it was held by the highest court that the trial could not be suspended indefinitely without violating the professor's right to a speedy trial. The Court was obviously aware of the adverse effects of the pending indictment, the public scorn, the possible deprivation of employment, and the curtailment of the professor's freedom of speech, of association, and perhaps the curtailment of his involvement in unpopular causes. A state cannot circumvent its Sixth Amendment obligation by postponing prosecution when the accused is in prison in another jurisdiction.[10] It should be observed that a nolle prosequi plea generally runs afoul of the right to a speedy trial, since the criminal case may be restored to the calendar at any time by a court order pursuant to the prosecutor's application to the court. If the nolle prosequi pleas is "with leave," it means that the court has already consented to reinstatement at a future date and the case can readily be restored for trial by the prosecutor without a court order.[11]

It is suffice to state, as did the U.S. Supreme Court in Pollard v. United States,[12] "whether delay in completing a prosecution . . . amounts to an unconstitutional deprivation of rights depends upon the circumstances."[13] And the circumstances in Whaley v. Rodriguez[14] were such that the police had exercised due diligence in attempting to find the criminal defendant, and that therefore none of the delay in finding him was chargeable to the state. A similar finding was made in People v. Gonzalez[15] where the defendant, charged with the criminal sale of a controlled substance, was not arrested on the spot because the undercover purchase of the drugs was part of a larger police investigation. When the police were ready to effect the arrest, the defendant could not be found for two years, as she used aliases and different apartments.

The sole issue before the court is whether the the two-year delay in arresting and prosecuting the defendant constituted a denial of due process necessitating dismissal of the indictment. This court finds that the defendant was not denied due process of law. As such, the defendants motion to dismiss the indictment is denied.

The burden of showing that there was not unreasonable pre-indictment delay in prosecuting a defendant is on the People. People v. Singer, 44 N.Y. 2d 24 (1975). The People have met that burden.

The determination of whether there has been a denial of a defendant's due process right as a result of unreasonable pre-indictment delay turns upon a balancing of several factors, including: the length of delay; the reason for delay; the degree of actual prejudice to the defendant; and the seriousness of the underlying offense. People v. Bonsauger, 91 A.D. 2d 1001, 457 N.Y.S. 2d 866.

Here we are dealing with a delay of under two years. The People have stated that they were unable to find the defendant during these two years. While, there is a testimony that the defendant had resided in the same area for over twenty-five years and that the defendant was arrested and briefly incarcerated in New York County, it appears from the record that the police exercised due diligence in their attempts to locate her. Det. Rivera made numerous trips to the defendant's neighborhood. There, he spoke to various individuals in an effort to ascertain the defendant's whereabouts. He also enlisted the aid of various informants in his search. . . . This is a serious crime. It involves the widespread distribution of narcotics on the streets of New York. The defendant has not demonstrated any potential impairment of her defense due to the delay. People v. Hoskins, 95 A.D. 2d 899, 464 N.Y.S. 2d 55. This court is not satisfied that the pre-indictment delay would in any way cloud the defendants recollection or undermine her defense. The defendant's motion to dismiss is denied. The aforesaid constitutes the opinion, decision and order of this court.

4.2 DELAY GENERALLY: REASONS AND WAIVER

The amorphous quality of the right to a speedy trial makes for litigation; but delays without fixed points in the process simply may go by without judicial intervention. It is frequently impossible to determine a precise point in time for purposes of denial or of waiver of the right to a speedy trial.[16] The Second U.S. Court of Appeals in the United States v. LoFranco[17] found that the criminal defendant had waived his right to a speedy trial by his plea of guilty; the claim of a speedy trial violation is non-jurisdictional and is waived by the guilty plea, despite the court's questioning of the exclusion of a significant period of time from the computation of the speedy trial period. More than a month later the same federal appellate court in United States v. Roman[18] ruled that the seventy-day speedy trial exclusion applied to the original indictment as well as to the superseding indictment that contained charges which, under the double jeopardy principles, are required to be joined with the original charges.

Statutes of limitations are also the criminal defendant's safeguard against prejudice from delay, but generally the defendant must (in order to win on the statute of limitations issue) prove that the delay resulted in actual prejudice and that it was intentional and improperly motivated.[19] Delay allegedly caused by loss or scattering of witnesses,[20] impairment of witnesses' memories,[21] or loss of evidence,[22] for example, may not be sufficient to invoke the Sixth Amendment protection. Such excusable conduct, however, is not necessarily matched by delay due to congested dockets and understaffed prosecutors, the point being that the ultimate responsibility for speedy trial rests upon the shoulders of the prosecution.[23] A criminal defendant successful in protecting his right to a speedy trial must take the initiative in asserting his/her right.[24] Prejudice to the defendant by delay is weighed in light of the need to protect him/her against oppressive pre-trial incarceration, uncertainty and anxiety, and impairment of his/her defense.[25]

It should be noted that denial of a motion to dismiss based upon delay which amounts to deprivation of the right to a speedy trial is not appealable before the actual trial, since it lacks the finality indispensable to appellate review.[26]

4.3 TIME COMPUTATION AND TIME ANALYSIS

In computing the seventy-day period of time under the Speedy Trial Act of 1974[27] the Second U.S. Court of Appeals ruled that any delay caused by pre-trial motion after a hearing but before the federal district court received all the submissions by counsel that the court needed to decide the motion (and an additional thirty days once the motion is actually taken under advisement by the court) is excluded.[28] (The U.S. Supreme Court in Henderson v. United States[29] had earlier given its blessings to that time computation.) The excludable time was apparently warranted in this international drug-smuggling and money-laundering case, and the federal appellate court found no abuse of discretion in the trial judge's tolling of the speedy-trial clock to enable new assistant prosecutors to prepare for trial after the ill health of the chief prosecutor.

In the Matter of Vincent M.[30] was decided by the New York Appellate Division, First Dept., by invoking a New York rule on time computation for purposes of ruling on the speedy trial guarantee. Here the defendant was indicted for robbery before his sixteenth birthday, and the case was removed to the Family Court. The assistant district attorneys thereupon requested various adjournments for the next 161 days, and the defendant ultimately moved to dismiss the case for the government's failure to accord him a speedy trial. The court agreed with the defendant:

It is uncontroverted that defendant did not receive a fact-finding hearing within the initial prescribed period of 60 days nor within the 90-day period allowed upon a showing of 'good cause,' nor were 'special circumstances' shown to excuse the delay beyond 90 days. In fact, 161 days passed after the initial appearance without commencement of the fact-finding hearing. The circumstances which led to the multiplicity of adjournments granted to the district attorney . . . did not constitute 'good cause' or 'special circumstances' within the meaning of the statute.[31]

The court opined that the government's argument that ''invocation of these speedy trial provisions would lead to widespread dismissal of delinquency cases'' was simply not the case.[32] But less than eight months later the New York Court of Appeals in In Matter of Frank C.[33] did just that, after finding a 217-day delay in the trial of a juvenile charged with possession of a controlled substance:

While no specific provision for dismissal is made in the statute . . . the statute's specific and mandatory language, as well as its precise deadlines and clear legislative history, lead to the conclusion that the Legislature did not intend to leave the sanction for non-compliance to the Family Court's discretion. Rather, a holding mandating dismissal of the charges seems necessary to effectuate the legislative goal of prompt adjudication and to ensure consistency in the statute's application.[34]

The U.S. Supreme Court in 1970 reviewed a conviction of a defendant who had been extradited to Florida and convicted after a delay of eight years; the highest court proclaimed that the long delay was ''intolerable as a matter of fact and impermissible as a matter of law'' in view of the actual prejudice created by the long delay in the death of witnesses and the loss of police records.[35] The Court observed that the defendant's interest in a speedy trial was matched by society's interest in prompt resolution of pending criminal charges; delays diminish a

prosecution's case, especially in face of the likely impeachment of
testimony.[36] Swift justice also serves as a deterrent to official abuse
and lawlessness.[37] The highest court in United States v. Marion,[38]
however, was technically accurate in refusing to dismiss a criminal
case after a delay of three years between the end of a criminal scheme
and the return of the indictment; the speedy trial concept, according
to the Court, does not arise until the accused is indicted or arrested.
A similar view is evident in Dillingham v. United States[39] where a
lapse of twenty-two months between arrest and indictment and a twelve-
month lapse between indictment and trial were deemed not necessarily
crucial on the issue of speedy trial; the pre-indictment delay did not
count, absent a showing of actual prejudice to the defendant, only the
time between arrest and indictment being countable for speedy trial
computation.[40]

4.4 PRE-TRIAL DETENTION GENERALLY

In United States v. Salerno[41] and in United States v. Cafaro[42] the
U.S. Supreme Court in early summer of 1987 upheld the constitutionality of jailing defendants who had not been convicted of crimes.[43]
The policy justification for imprisonment was the need to control or
regulate "organized crime" in the United States. The pre-trial detention provisions of the Bail Reform Act of 1984[44] were the basis for
upholding the pre-trial detentions. Under the Act the defendant may
be incarcerated if the government proves by clear and convincing evidence, after an adversary hearing, that no bail conditions "will reasonably assure . . . the safety of any other person and the community." The Act apparently applies only to repeat offenders or to those
charged with crimes of violence, capital crimes, or serious drug offenses. According to the highest court, "the government's interest in
community safety can, in appropriate circumstances, outweigh the individual's liberty interest." The Court found no fault with the pre-trial
detention violating the Eighth Amendment's ban on excessive bail; the
Eighth Amendment provides no right to bail and bail is not available
for capital offenses, according to the Court. The dissent of Justice
Marshall pointed out that the pre-trial detention undermined the presumption of innocence of the defendant:

Under this Act an untried indictment somehow acts to permit a detention based
on other charges, which after an acquittal would be unconstitutional. The con-

clusion is inescapable that the indictment has been turned into evidence, if not that the defendant is guilty of the crime charged, then that left to his own devices he will soon be guilty of something else.''

Shortly thereafter, in July 1987, in Williams v. Ward[45] the federal District Court for the Southern District of New York set a twenty-four-hour deadline for a judicial determination that probable cause existed for an arrest without a warrant. The court's rationale was found in the Fourth Amendment's right to be free of unreasonable seizures; the court's ire stemmed from the fact that there had been ''an increase in the number of courtrooms and court personnel involved in the arrest and arraignment processes'' in the city of New York.[46] But in August 1987 the Second U.S. Court of Appeals in United States v. Coonan[47] carved out an exception to the requirement that a hearing be held within five days if the government is seeking pre-trial detention of the defendant. The exception occurs where the defendant is already in jail for another crime, for then bail is not an issue and an immediate hearing is not necessary.

The Illinois Supreme Court decision in People v. Goins[48] involved the question as to when the speedy trial period began; the defendant was indicted and jailed in one county for residential burglarly and then moved to a second county where the crime occurred and where he was jailed. The court ruled that the speedy trial period began when he was jailed in the first county, even though it was the second county that had jurisdiction over his offense. The court observed that the Illinois legislature had intended a distinction between jurisdiction and venue to run throughout the Illinois criminal law including the speedy trial provision.

4.5 THE SPEEDY TRIAL ACT OF 1974

In sharp contrast to the judicially created balancing test which the courts apply in speedy trial claims under the Sixth Amendment,[49] the Speedy Trial Act of 1974[50] established specific time limits between various stages of all federal criminal trial proceedings.[51] Under the Act, federal authorities must file an information or indictment within thirty days of the date of defendant's arrest or within thirty days of service of the summons on the defendant.[52] If the defendant enters a plea of not guilty, the trial must commence within seventy days from the filing date of the information or indictment, or within seventy days from the date the defendant appeared before a judicial officer of the court in which the charge is pending, whichever is later.[53] But in any event trial must begin within ninety days of the date the government detains a defendant solely to await trial or designates a released person awaiting trial as a high risk.[54] A court may not hold such a detainee in custody pending trial after the ninety-day period expires.[55] On the other hand, trial may not begin in fewer than thirty days from the date the defendant appears before the court pro se or through counsel, unless the defendant consents in writing to an earlier trial date.[56] Interestingly, Section 3161(h) of the Act provides that certain types of delays are excluded from the computation of time expired, to wit: delays that result from other proceedings involving the defendant,[57] delays attributed to the absence or unavailability of the defendant or of an essential witness;[58] or delays caused by joinder with a co-defendant for whom the time for trial has not yet elapsed.[59] A trial judge has the discretion to exclude delays attributable to any continuance that is granted in order to serve the ends of justice, which may mean that the public interests outweigh the defendant's interest in a speedy trial,[60] provided that the court enters its reasons for doing so in the official record of the court.[61]

Obviously, should the government not adhere to the specific time limits, the case must be dismissed,[62] but the defendant bears the burden of proof of the government's non-compliance with the provisions of the act.[63] Failure of the defendant to assert his rights under the act may constitute a waiver of his right to dismissal of the case.[64]

It should be noted that both the Juvenile Justice and Delinquency Prevention Act[65] and the Interstate Agreement on Detainers Act[66] contain speedy trial provisions, the latter establishing maximum time periods between the various stages of pre-trial proceedings and the former requiring dismissal of information or indictment if the juvenile is detained longer than 30 days prior to trial, unless the delay is caused by the juvenile and consented to by defense counsel in the interests of justice.[67] The Interstate Agreement on Detainers Act mandates dismissal if the trial does not commence within 180 days of a prisoner's request for trial on charges pending in another jurisdiction, although the trial court may grant a necessary or reasonable continuance for good cause.[68]

In 1988 the Second U.S. Court of Appeals had occasion to consider an unusual plea under the Speedy Trial Act of 1974. The defendant, a citizen of Greece, was indicted in 1984 for tax frauds, and two years later he moved to dismiss the indictment. But he had never appeared to answer the charges since he was in Greece and was not subject to extradition to the United States. He contended, nevertheless, that the U.S. government failed to exercise due diligence in seeking extradition as a matter of comity! The federal appellate court opined that "compelling the government to consider making . . . an exception . . . would vitiate the policy and render meaningless 'our traditional deference to the judgment of the executive department in matters of foreign policy'. . . . Due diligence does not require the government to pursue that which is futile. Given the deference we must give to a coordinate branch of government, particularly to the executive branch in matters of foreign policy, we hold that the speedy trial clause does not prevent the government from adhering to its general policy not to seek extradition as a matter of comity.''[69]

Despite a five-year delay in coming to trial in United States v. Oliver[70] the federal district court upheld an indictment charging a $1.7 million counterfeiting scheme. Initially, the charges of possessing and manufacturing counterfeit money were dismissed because the prosecution had failed to obtain an indictment within thirty days following arrest of the three men as required by the Speedy Trial Act. But five years later the grand jury voted an indictment related to the same underlying alleged counterfeiting, and the court sustained that indictment because "the crimes currently charged are different and require different proof than those charged in the original complaint." It should be noted that in United States v. Napolitano[71] the Speedy Trial Act was held not to take a sweeping "criminal episode" approach which would bar the prosecution from raising any charge in a subsequent indictment arising from the facts underlying the initial complaint.

The Interstate Agreement on Detainers,[72] it should be noted, has been involved in countless episodes, including the time that a criminal defendant spends at a correctional institution as opposed to a jail. In People v. Reilly[73] the New York court ruled that the defendant did not begin serving his federal sentence until subsequent to the time when he was transported to the correctional institution.

NOTES

1. See United States v. Marion, 404 US 307 (1971) at 320.
2. The Fifth Amendment provides that "no person shall . . . be deprived of life, liberty, or property, without due process of law. . . . "
3. 18 USC App 545 (1982).
4. Section 48(b) thereof and also Section 50(b) thereof.
5. 18 USC 3161–3174.
6. Note that Section 3161 thereof specifies time limits between arrest, indictment, and trial and acceptable delays within each period.
7. _____AD2d_____, _____NYS2d_____ (October 22, 1987).
8. Id.
9. 386 US 213 (1966), rev'g 145 SE2d 909 (N.C., 1979).
10. See Smith v. Hooey, 393 US 374 (1968); also note Case & Comment (July–August 1986) at 14.
11. Infra notes 9 and 10.
12. 352 US 354 (1957).
13. Id. at 361.
14. _____F2d_____ (2nd Cir., February 22, 1988).
15. _____NYS2d_____ (NY County, February 23, 1988).
16. Note Barker v. Wingo, 407 US 514 (1972).
17. _____F2d_____ (2nd Cir., May 6, 1987).
18. _____F2d_____ (2nd Cir., June 22, 1987).
19. Note United States v. Lovasco, 431 US 783 (1977).
20. See Stoner v. Graddick, 751 F2d 1535 (11th Cir., 1985).
21. See United States v. Marler, 756 F2d 206 (1st Cir., 1985).
22. Infra note 18.
23. See Strunk v. United States, 412 US 434 (1973).
24. Infra note 14.
25. Infra notes 10 and 14.
26. See Abney v. United States, 431 US 651 (1977); furthermore, the pretrial appeal must be separated from the principle issues of the pending trial.
27. Infra note 5.
28. See United States v. Ditommaso, _____F2d_____ (2nd Cir., April 20, 1987).
29. 106 S Ct 1871 (1986).
30. _____AD2d_____, _____NYS2d_____ (February 24, 1987).
31. According to the court,

Family Court Act §310.2 expressly provides that: "After a petition has been filed, the respondent is entitled to a speedy fact-finding hearing." The term "speedy" as used in this section is spelled out in various other sections of the Family Court Act which set specific time limits governing each stage of a delinquency proceeding. Thus, Family Court Act §340.1 reads in pertinent part:

§340.1 Time of fact-finding hearing . . .

2. If the respondent is not in detention the fact-finding hearing shall commence not more than sixty days after the conclusion of the initial appearance except as provided in subdivision three.

3. The court may adjourn a fact-finding hearing:

(a) on its own motion or on motion of the presentment agency for good cause shown for not more than three days if the respondent is in detention and not more than thirty days if the respondent is not in detention; provided, however, that if there is probable cause to believe the respondent committed a homicide or a crime which resulted in a person being incapacitated from attending court, the court may adjourn the hearing for a reasonable length of time; or

(b) on motion by the respondent for good cause shown for not more than thirty days; or

(c) on its own motion for not more than six months if the proceeding has been adjourned in contemplation of dismissal pursuant to §315.3.

4. The court shall state on the record the reasons for any adjournment of the fact-finding hearing.

5. Successive motions to adjourn a fact-finding hearing shall not be granted in the absence of a showing, on the record, of special circumstances; such circumstances shall not include calendar congestion or the status of the court's docket or backlog.

Although the provisions of the Criminal Procedure Law do not apply to juvenile delinquency proceedings unless specifically prescribed (Family Ct Act §303.1[1]), the Family Court may consider judicial interpretations of the Criminal Procedure Law as an aid in interpreting similar provisions of the Family Court Act. Accordingly, appellant analogizes Family Court Act §310.2 to CPL 30.20, which sets forth the right to a speedy trial without giving explicit time limitations, citing *People v. Taranovich* (37 NY 2d 442) for its position that respondent's right to a speedy trial was not violated.

However, in *Taranovich* the criminal action was commenced prior to the effective date of CPL 30.30, which provided for specific time periods. Thus, the Court of Appeals, in that case, decided the defendant was not deprived of his constitutional right to a speedy trial. It enumerated five factors to be considered in evaluating such a claim. While respondent did not expressly appeal any violation of his constitutional right to a speedy trial, the speedy trial provisions in the Family Court Act are "rights . . . *in addition* to those already vested by the Constitution." (*Matter of J.V.* , 127 Misc 2d 780, 782, emphasis added.)

We further agree with the Family Court herein, which found that: "The plain language of Family Court Act §340.1 places the onus on the court to commence fact finding within a prescribed limit with no provision for excluding periods from computing time . . . " (*Accord, Matter of Steven C.*, 129 Misc 2d 946; but see, *Matter of Rodney M.*, 130 Misc 2d 928.).

32.

Family Court Act §340.1 allows successive adjournments in "special circumstances." It also permits adjournments for "a reasonable length of time" where there is probable cause to believe the respondent committed a homicide or a crime resulting in a person being incapacitated from attending court. This affords flexibility to Family Court judges presented with motions involving speedy trial violations. In addition, we note that dismissal for such violations is never automatic but lies in the discretion of the court. We emphasize that the Family Court properly exercised that discretion in this case where 161 days had elapsed without commencement of the fact-finding hearing and without a satisfactory excuse for such delay, i.e., "special circumstances," established in the record by the presentment agency.

The sanction of dismissal, although "more serious than an exclusionary rule or reversal for a new trial," is the "only possible remedy" for such egregious violation of the speedy trial right (see, *Barker v. Wingo*, 407 US 514, 522). Moreover, the Legislature has provided the remedy of dismissal if a respondent's rights under §310.2 are denied (Family Ct Act §332.1[8]). In similar cases, we have upheld such dismissal for failure to comply with this speedy trial mandate (*Matter of Robert G.*, 120 AD 2d 997; *Matter of Frank Clay*, 121 AD 2d 266, *lv to app den* ____NY 2d____, Jan. 15, 1987).

Accordingly, the order of the Family Court, New York County (*Mortimer Getzels, J.*) entered Jan. 3, 1986, granting respondent Vincent M.'s motion to dismiss the petition, should be affirmed, without costs and without disbursements.

All concur.

33.   ____NY2d____ NE2d (October 13, 1987).

34. See Sections 310.2 and 332.1 (8) of New York Family Court Act. According to the court,

the "speedy hearing" provision at issue here was enacted in 1982 as part of a sweeping overhaul of the procedures governing juvenile delinquency proceedings (L 1982, ch 920 [codified as article 3 of the Family Court Act, §§301.1–385.2]). The purpose of the amendment package as a whole was to reflect the significant changes in the legal rights of juveniles that have occurred since the late 1960s and to standardize practice throughout the state (Bill Jacket, L 1982, ch 920, Memorandum in Support of A 7974-A; *see*, M. Sobie, Practice Commentary, *supra*, Family Ct Act, art 3, pp. 258–262). Among the most important aspects of the revised procedural rules were the various provisions establishing specific time limitations to govern each stage of the proceeding from arrest through final dispositions (*see e.g.*, Family Ct. Act §§307.1, 302.2, 332.1, 340.1, 350.1; *see also* Sobie, Practice Commentaries, *supra*, pp. 261–262, 330–331). The stated purpose of these provisions was to assure swift and certain adjudication at all phases of the delinquency proceeding (*see*, Bill Jacket, *supra*, Memorandum in Support of A 7974-A), a concern which we recognized in *People ex rel. Guggenheim v. Mucci* (32 NY2d 307).

Viewed in this light, §340.1 leaves no room for the contention that delays outside of the presentment agency's control should not provide a basis for the remedy of dismissal. Unlike CPL 30.30, Family Court Act 340.1 is a true "speedy trial" provision, in that both its language and its underlying purpose are directed toward bringing the accused juvenile to trial within a specified sixty- to ninety-day period (barring "special circumstances"). Indeed, the legislative decision expressly to preclude "court congestion" and other docket problems as permissible grounds for successive adjournments furnishes a clear indication that in adopting section 340.1 the Legislature meant to address all of the sources of delay within the system and not just those connected with the presentment agency. Moreover, the fact that the Legislature enacted the statute despite the concerns expressed by some regarding the undue burden its strict time limitations would impose on the Family Court system (see, Bill Jacket, L 1982, ch 920, Office of Court Administration, Memorandum; id., Association of Judges of the Family Court of the State of New York, Memorandum in Opertion) strongly suggests that the Legislature weighed all of the competing considerations and found the goal of speedy resolution charges against juveniles to be paramount.

Finally, although the appellant presentment agency argues otherwise, it is not necessary to "borrow" the remedy provided for in CPL 30.30 in order to conclude that a violation of Family Court Act §340.10 must lead to dismissal. While no specific provision for dismissal is made in the statute (cf. Family Ct Act §32.1 [8] [contemplating dismissal as a remedy for violation of Family Ct Act §310.2's general speedy hearing requirement]), the statute's specific and mandatory language, as well as its precise deadlines and clear legislative history, lead to the conclusion tht the Legislature did not intend to leave the sanction for noncompliance to the Family Court's discretion. Rather, a holding mandating dismissal of the charges seems necessary to effectuate the legislative goal of prompt adjudication and to ensure consistency in the statute's application.

This is not to suggest that §340.1 automatically requires dismissal in all cases in which the sixty-day time limitation genuinely cannot be met. To the contrary, the Legislature built a degree of flexibility into the statute by providing for adjournments in the event of "good cause shown" or "special circumstances." Since the parties in this appeal have not claimed that these statutory tests for permissible adjournments were satisfied here, we do not consider the precise scope of these terms. We note, however, that whether a particular event or set of events constitutes "good cause" or "special circumstances"—obviously, a more stringent standard—is a matter that must be decided on a case-by-case basis, with due regard to the stated legislative goal of prompt adjudication. Requests for adjournments should always be considered in light of the statutory standards, and the court's conclusions should be stated briefly on the record so that the propriety of various delays can later be assessed by reviewing court (see also Family Ct Act §340.1 [5]).

In this instance, some 217 days elapsed since the date of respondent's initial appearance without a fact-finding hearing having been held. Inasmuch as the adjournments were not based on any claimed "good cause" or "special circumstance," the trial court correctly dismissed the petition. Accordingly, the order of the Appellate Division, which affirmed the trial court's dismissal order should be affirmed.

35. See Dickey v. Florida, 398 US 30 (1970).
36. See Flanagan v. United States, 465 US 259 (1984).
37. Infra note 33.
38. 404 US 307 (1971).
39. 423 US 64 (1975).

40. See Barker v. Wingo, infra note 14.
41. _____US_____ (1987).
42. _____US_____ (1987).
43. See A.B.A.J. (August 1, 1987) at 54.
44. 18 USC 3142(e).
45. _____F Supp_____ (SDNY, July 2, 1987).
46. The court relied on a 1975 U.S. Supreme Court ruling, Gerstein v. Pugh, 402 US 103 (1975), which held that suspects must be produced for a "probable cause" hearing within "a brief period" after detention begins. See *New York Times* (July 7, 1987) at B1 et seq and also *New York Times* (July 13, 1987) at A13.
47. _____F2d_____ (2nd Cir., August 19, 1987). According to the court, to do otherwise would create a "rigid system that would require meaningless and unwanted hearings, that would protect liberty interests that are slim if not illusory, and that would allow defense attorneys to frustrate the functioning of the Act itself (as arguably, if unintentionally, happened here)."
48. _____NE2d_____ (Ill., January 19, 1988).
49. See Sections 4.1, 4.2, and 4.4 herein.
50. 18 USC 3161 to 3174 (1982).
51. See United States v. Shahryar, 719 F2d 1522 (11th Cir., 1983).
52. 18 USC 3161(b) (1982).
53. 18 USC 3161(c)(1) (1982).
54. 18 USC 3164(a)–(b) (1982).
55. 18 USC 3164(c) (1982).
56. 18 USC 3161(c)(2) (1982).
57. 18 USC 3161(h)(1) (1982).
58. See United States v. Garrett, 720 F2d 705 (DC Cir., 1983), cert den 456 US 1037 (1984).
59. 18 USC 3161(h)(7) (1982).
60. Note United States v. Norton, 755 F2d 1428 (11th Cir., 1985).
61. 18 USC 3161 (h)(8)(A) (1982).
62. Note 18 USC 3162(a)(2) (1982).
63. See generally United States v. Fielding, 645 F2d 719 (9th Cir., 1981).
64. 18 USC 3162(a)(1)–(2) (1982).
65. 18 USC 5031 to 5042 (1982).
66. 18 USC App 545 (1982).
67. 18 USC 5036 (1982).
68. _____F2d_____ (2nd Cir., January 15, 1988):

In defining the contours of the Sixth Amendment's due diligence requirement in this case, our prior decision in *United States v. Salzmann* [548 F2d 395, 2d Cir, 1976] is instructive. In *Salzmann* we affirmed the dismissal of an indictment for failure by the government to exercise due diligence to obtain the defendant's presence for trial. The defendant in that case was a Vietnam war draft evader living in Israel who was indicted for violations of the Selective Service Act. He moved to dismiss the indictment based upon the speedy trial rules then in effect in this circuit. The district court granted the motion, and we affirmed, but to respond to his "intimation" that a reason for his refusal to return to the United States was his financial inability to do so, the government was not duly diligent in attempting to obtain his presence for trial.

Although this court did not have occasion in *Salzmann* to determine whether the government should have prevailed upon Israel to deport the defendant, Judge Kaufman in his majority opinion in *Salzmann* did express in *dicta* the court's sense of what due diligence would require of the government in seeking the return of a fugitive who was not subject to extradition by treaty. Specifically, the majority indicated that a

> *considered refusal* on the part of the Government to seek return of selective service offenders [would not violate] standards of due diligence . . . in those instances where no right of extradition exists by treaty . . . Where the United States must rely solely on comity . . . ,diplomatic factors may properly be taken into account in determining what diligence is due. We are unpersuaded that under these circumstances, the United States was obliged to seek Salzmann's return by means dehors the extradition treaty. . . . 548 F. 2d at 402 (emphasis added).

In a concurring opinion, Judge Feinberg agreed with the majority that the government's failure to offer Salzmann financial assistance necessitated the dismissal of the indictment. Judge Feinberg also concluded, however, that because the government "did nothing" to seek defendant's forcible return to his country, it failed to demonstrate the necessary diligence in order to avoid dismissal of the indictment. Judge Feinberg thus would have required the government at least to pursue efforts to seek the return of the defendant.

Relying on Judge Feinberg's concurring opinion, Diacolios argues that the government had an obligation to inquire of the State Department whether or not a policy decision was made concerning the extradition of Greek nationals. The district court appeared to accept this argument in reflecting its dissatisfaction with Assistant U.S. Attorney's explanation for declining to take steps to obtain Diacolios' extradition. We agree with Judge Haight that the mere assertion of "general" policy not to seek extradition [sic] is insufficient by itself to satisfy the government's obligation of due diligence. Nevertheless, we believe that subsequent information provided to the district court by the government confirmed the existence of a considered policy decision regarding extradition of Greek nationals. Consequently, we do not read Salzmann to require in this case anything more of the government than to determine whether Diacolios was subject to extradition in light of the State Department's "general" policy.

69. _____F Supp_____ (EDNY, 1988).

70. 761 F2d 135 (2d Cir, 1985).
71. Infra note 66.
72.

The Interstate Agreement on Detainers (CPL 580.20) is a compact among 48 States, the District of Columbia, the Virgin Islands and the United States (see, *Carchman v. Nash*, 473 US 716; 2 Waxner, New York Criminal Practice, §10.23; Fried, *The Interstate Agreement on Detainers and the Federal Government*, 6 Hofstra L Rev 493 [1978]). New York adopted this compact in 1957 (L 1957 ch 440 [eff. Sept 1, 1957]) and Congress entered into the IAD on behalf of the United States and the District of Columbia in 1970 (Pub L No 91-538, 84 US Stat. 1397).

Article IV of the IAD (CPL 580.20 [IV]) provides that a prosecutor of a "[r]eceiving state" (CPL 580.20 [11] [c]) (in the present case, New York) "shall be entitled" to the production of a prisoner held in another State (or the United States) "upon presentation of a written request for temporary custody [of the prisoner]" (CPL 580.20 [IV] [a]). However, there are certain conditions attached to the exercise of this right. First, the prisoner must be actually "serving a term of imprisonment" at the time the request is made. Second, a detainer must previously have been lodged against the prisoner. Third, the state court in which the charges are pending must "have approved, recorded and transmitted the request [for temporary custody]." Fourth, the Governor of the State in which the defendant is imprisoned must be given at least 30 days during which he may refuse to release the prisoner.

First, we determine that the defendant was not "serving a term of imprisonment" within the meaning of Article IV(a) of the IAD (CPL 580.20 [IV] [a]) at the time that his production in State court was first obtained. For this reason alone, the time constraints of Article IV(c) of the IAD do not apply.

18 USC former §3568, repealed effective Nov. 1, 1987 pursuant to §235 of Pub. L. 98-473, provided: "the sentence of imprisonment of any person convicted of an offense shall commence to run from the date on which such person is received at the penitentiary, reformatory, or jail for service of sentence*** If any such person shall be committed to a jail or other place of detention to await transportation to the place at which his sentence is to be served, his sentence shall commence to run from the date on which he is received at such jail or other place of detention."

Although this language may suggest that the defendant must be deemed to have begun serving his Federal sentence as soon as it was imposed, because he was thereupon committed to the custody of the Metropolitan Correctional Center to await transportation to a federal penitentiary, we agree with the court in *Lublin v. Johnson* (628 F Supp 1496 [EDNY1986]) which held that such an interpretation would not be consonant with the policies underlying the IAD. In Lublin v. Johnson (supra, at 1499-1500) the court stated that "'(t)he IAD was enacted for a specific and limited purpose: the minimization of interference 'with a prisoner's treatment and rehabilitation.' *United States ex rel. Esola v. Groomes*, 520 F 2d 830, 833. A detainer lodged against a prisoner can affect adversely a prisoner's treatment and rehabilitation only upon his entry into the assigned facility. Accordingly, petitioner began serving a term of imprisonment upon formally entering the Lewisberg Federal Facility*** and not on the effective date of sentencing under §3568 [of Title 18 of the United States Code]" (citing *United States v. Wilson*,

719 F2d 1491, 1494–1495, n 1; see also, *Crooker v. United States*, 814 F 2d 75, 77–78; *United States v. Glasgow*, 790 F 2d 446, 448–450, *cert denied* 475 US 1124; *Matter of Cresong v. Nevil*, 51 AD 2d 1096).

73. _____AD2d_____, _____NYS2d_____ (2nd Dept, April 4, 1988).

5

Fairness Criteria for the Fair Criminal Trial

5.1 PLEAS IN THE CRIMINAL COURT

Fairness in the criminal trial may, in part, result from the nature of the very plea entered by the accused or criminal defendant. The Federal Rules of Criminal Procedure permit a criminal defendant to enter a plea of guilty,[1] a plea of not guilty,[2] or a nolo contendere plea.[3] The guilty plea is an admission of all the elements of the crime charged, and is made knowingly and voluntarily.[4] The nolo contendere plea requires the consent of the court,[5] and has the effect of a guilty plea since it admits every essential element of the crime;[6] a defendant who pleads nolo contendere waives his right to a jury trial.[7] Unlike a plea of guilty, a plea of nolo contendere is inadmissible as evidence of guilt in subsequent civil litigation arising from the same act or conduct.[8] The nolo contendere plea requires that it be entered by the defendant knowingly and voluntarily.[9]

It should be noted that a plea of not guilty accompanied by stipulations to incriminatory facts resembles both a guilty plea and nolo contendere plea because the defendant waives many of his rights under the Fifth Amendment and under the Sixth Amendment.[10] However, that defendant might still confront witnesses or challenge non-jurisdictional matters on appeal, or in fact present his defenses.[11]

Where the defendant refuses to enter a plea, Rule 11(a) of the Federal Rules of Criminal Procedure requires the federal district court to enter a plea of not guilty. Before accepting a guilty plea, the court must be sure that the defendant is competent to enter that plea;[12] indeed, a competency hearing is required whenever there is "reasonable cause to believe the accused is insane or so mentally incompetent as to be unable to understand the proceedings against him or to assist in his own defense."[13] In United States v. Peeler[14] the Eighth U.S. Court of Appeals held the defendant competent to stand trial despite the testimony of both court-appointed psychiatrists that the defendant was not rational enough to understand legal proceedings and to assist in his own defense; defendant's attorney had advised the court that the defendant was capable of changing his plea to guilty. Note that the standard of competency required to enter a plea of guilty is the same standard of competency required to stand trial.[15] In United States v. Hollis[16] the same court had previously found another defendant competent to stand trial, because the defendant cooperated with his attorney in the preparation of his defense, had no previous psychiatric treatment, exhibited no signs of mental instability, and the psychiatric report stated that defendant was competent.

5.2 NOTICE TO USE INCULPATORY STATEMENT

The fairness of the criminal trial may well depend upon proper notice to use inculpatory statement, as illustrated by the two New York decisions of People v. Boughton[17] and People v. O'Doherty,[18] decided on November 24, 1987, by the New York Court of Appeals. Section 710.30 of the Civil Practice law requires that the prosecutor serve upon a defendant within fifteen days after arraignment notice of intention to offer at trial evidence of statements made by the defendant to public servants. But subparagraph (2) thereof permits the prosecutor to serve a late notice "for good cause." In the absence of a timely notice or an approved late notice, the evidence may not be received against the defendant at trial, unless the defendant has nevertheless made an unsuccessful suppression notice directed at such evidence.[19] In the O'Doherty case the highest New York court found that the State of New York "did not establish good cause for the delay, and that, therefore, it was error to permit them to serve a late notice and to admit such evidence at defendant's trial."[20] The court added that "lack of prejudice to the defendant resulting from the delay does not obviate the need for the People to meet the statutory requirement of good cause before they may be permitted to serve a late notice."[21] The origin of the rule on admissions or even confessions of the defendant, according to the court, is found in Jackson v. Denno[22] "in which the U.S. Supreme Court held that such statements may not be considered by a jury which is to adjudicate guilt or innocence, unless there has first been a determination by a separate fact finder, following an evidentiary hearing, that such statements were made voluntarily." The New York court opined that "not only considerations of fairness to the defendant, but also concerns for the efficient conduct of criminal prosecutions underlie" the New York statute; that the exclusionary sanction for failure to comply with Section 710.30(3) of CPL "reflects a judgment that the loss of the use of the evidence is an acceptable price to pay to achieve the desired goals."[23]

In the Boughton case[24] the same New York Court of Appeals held that "the prosecutor's notice of intent to introduce a statement must be made within the time prescribed by the statute, unless good cause is shown for the delay and mere neglect is no excuse. . . . In this case the defendant did not receive effective notice until after the time had run. The prior notice, although timely served, had been withdrawn, and thus was ineffective. Accordingly, the statement should have been excluded."

5.3 EVIDENCE OF PRIOR BAD ACTS
OR PRIOR CRIMES

The basic fairness of the criminal trial might in most cases be dependent upon the exclusion of evidence of the defendant's prior bad acts or prior crimes. In Huddleston v. United States[25] the Sixth U.S. Court of Appeals, however, opined that introduction of evidence that the defendant (charged with possessing stolen videotapes) sold television sets to a storeowner for only $28 each did not violate the defendant's fair trial rights; such evidence was admissible since the trial court had determined that there was a preponderance of evidence to show that the defendant committed that prior bad act.

In civil actions evidence of the defendant's prior bad acts or prior crimes is not admissible under Rule 404(b) of the Federal Rules of Evidence.[26] However, such evidence is admissible as proof of a matter in issue such as motive, intent, or absence of mistake or accident.

In a proceeding under the civil rights statute of 18 USC 1983 (which

approximates criminal rights) the First U.S. Court of Appeals in Lataille v. Ponte.[27] excluded evidence of the plaintiff-prisoner's disciplinary record, even though it was offered to show knowledge, motive, and opportunity. Plaintiff's civil rights action against six prison
guards alleged that plaintiff was beaten while he was housed in a seg-
regation unit. Defendants contended that plaintiff was the aggressor,
and that plaintiff's disciplinary record attested to many assaults, hos-
tage takings, weapons possessions, fire settings, and attempted es-
capes. The trial court permitted defendants to cross-examine plaintiff
on the entire disciplinary record, but the record itself was denied admissibility; the jury verdict favored the defendants. The federal appellate court agreed on the non-admissibility of the disciplinary record,
and reversed the jury verdict because "it was abundantly clear that the
evidence of Lataille's prior disciplinary offenses was offered by defendants and admitted by the district court for the purpose of showing
that Lataille was a violent person and that he, therefore, must have
been the aggressor and precipitated the assault. The evidence was clearly
inadmissible under Rule 404.''

5.4 ADMISSIONS AGAINST INTEREST
OF DEFENDANT

In United States v. Dohm[28] the Fifth U.S. Court of Appeals had
held that incriminating statements made by a defendant at a pre-trial
hearing in the exercise of his Eighth Amendment right to a non-exces-
sive bail were admissible against him in his criminal trial. This position was contrary to a prior U.S. Supreme Court decision in Simmons
v. United States[29] that incriminating statements made by a defendant
in the exercise of his Fourth Amendment rights at a pre-trial suppression hearing were not admissible in his criminal trial, because a criminal defendant should not be forced to surrender one constitutional
right in order to assert another constitutional right.[30] The highest court
in effect thereby conferred "use immunity" on all testimony offered
by defendants in the exercise of their Fourth Amendment rights at such
hearings."Use immunity" renders evidence inadmissible but does not
preclude prosecution on the crime to which the inadmissible evidence
relates. "Use immunity" is distinct from "transactional immunity"
which attaches to persons rather than to evidence, precluding prosecution on stipulated crimes but leaving the prosecution free to use

evidence given by such an immunized person against him on other charges. Neither "use immunity" nor "transactional immunity" precludes the use of testimony for impeachment if the declarant takes the witness stand.[31] The dissenting opinion of Judge Goldbert in the Dohm case[32] catalogued innumerable instances where courts have refused to admit incriminating statements made by defendants during pre-trial hearings such as Sixth Amendment requests for appointed counsel.[33] On a rehearing in the Dohm case in 1980 the conviction was reversed[34] on the ground that the magistrate who conducted the bail hearing had not properly advised the defendant of his right to remain silent. The concurring opinion of Judge Tate pointed out that "forcing the defendant either to sit mute or to run the risk of imperiling his right not to take the stand at a subsequent trial inefficiently injects unnecessary formality and risk into what would be an informal pre-trial proceeding."[35]

The California Supreme Court in People v. Coleman[36] conferred "use immunity" on statements made by the defendant at a probation revocation hearing. The permissibility of a choice hinged upon the degree of procedural protection attending it, i.e., the procedural safeguards such as the reasonable doubt standard and the right of cross-examination afford defendants a tactical alternative to testifying.

5.5 PROSECUTORIAL MISCONDUCT

It is obvious that prosecutorial misconduct precludes fairness at the criminal trial, although the Sixth Amendment guarantees a criminal defendant only a fair trial, not a perfect trial.[37] In Darden v. Wainright[38] the highest court opined that the prosecutor's misconduct "so infected the trial with unfairness as to make the resulting conviction a denial of due process." Overzealous performance of duties by prosecutors can take many, many forms, including improper remarks during argument to the jury; in Berger v. United States[39] the highest court had observed that "the average jury, in a greater or less degree, had confidence that these obligations, which so plainly rest upon the prosecuting attorney, will be faithfully observed. Consequently, improper suggestions, insinuations, and especially assertions of personal knowledge are apt to carry much weight against the accused when they should properly carry none." Standards of conduct for prosecutors are delineated in the American Bar Association Standards for Criminal Justice:

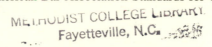

The Prosecution Function;[40] the National District Attorneys Association, National Prosecution Standards;[41] and the ABA Model Rules of Professional Conduct.[42] Rule 3.8 of the ABA Model Rules of Professional Conduct defines the "special responsibilities of a prosecutor," to wit:

The prosecutor in a criminal case shall (a) refrain from prosecuting a charge that the prosecutor knows is not supported by probable cause; (b) make reasonable efforts to assure that the accused has been advised of the right to, and the procedure for obtaining, counsel and has been given reasonable opportunity to obtain counsel; (c) not seek to obtain from an unrepresented accused a waiver of important pretrial rights, such as the right to a preliminary hearing; (d) make timely disclosure to the defense of all evidence or information known to the prosecutor that tends to negate the guilt of the accused or mitigates the offense, and, in connection with sentencing, disclose to the defense and to the tribunal all unprivileged information known to the prosecutor, except when the prosecutor is relieved of this responsibility by a protective order of this tribunal; and (e) exercise reasonable care to prevent investigators, law enforcement personnel, employees or other persons assisting or associated with the prosecutor in a criminal case from making an extrajudicial statement that the prosecutor would be prohibited from making under Rule 3.6. (on trial publicity)

Examples of prosecutorial misconduct are legion; the Florida Supreme Court in State v. Wheeler[43] reversed defendant's conviction for narcotics trafficking and firearm possession because the prosecutor told the jury in a closing argument that defendant was selling drugs that could eventually wind up on school grounds and in jurors' homes! The court deemed these remarks highly prejudicial and violative of the rule that a prosecutor cannot argue to the jury that the jurors may well be victims of defendant's behavior if the jurors fail to convict him.[44] (It should be noted that there was no evidence at trial that defendant ever sold narcotics that ended up on school grounds or in jurors' homes.) In State v. Smith[45] the prosecutor characterized the defense evidence as "lies" and "garbage" and implied that defendant's attorney had conceived lies which were presented to the court; the Ohio court held that these prejudicial remarks made a fair trial impossible. Prosecutorial closings that stress "law and order" themes urging jurors to send a message to the entire community that seeks a conviction have also been held to be improper.[46]

Public relations and trial publicity for the prosecutor can be a source of unfairness in the criminal trial. As stated in Rule 3.6 of the ABA Model Rules on Professional Responsibility, "a lawyer engaged in a case being tried to a jury shall not make an extrajudicial statement that a reasonable person would expect to be disseminated by means of mass public communication if the lawyer knows or reasonably should know that the statement will create a serious and imminent threat to the impartiality of the jury." In Berger v. United States,[47] more than fifty years ago, the U.S. Supreme Court wrote: "The U.S. Attorney is the representative not of an ordinary party to a controversy, but of a sovereignty whose obligation is to govern impartially . . . and whose interest therefore in a criminal prosecution is not that it shall win a case, but that justice shall be done. As such he is in a peculiar and very definite sense the servant of the law, the twofold aim of which is that guilt shall not escape nor innocence suffer."[48]

Prosecutorial bungling, however, did not deny the defendant in People v. Haupt[49] his right to a fair trial. Here the defendant alleged in 1983 that law enforcement officials had lost and destroyed evidence when he was indicted for murder in 1967;[50] but the New York court ruled that "any harm resulting from the loss of evidence over the 16-year period was negligible, and dismissal would be both disproportionately drastic and unnecessary in order to preserve the defendant's right to a fair trial."[51]

In the 1962 opinion of the U.S. Supreme Court in Wood v. Georgia[52] "the right of the courts to conduct their business" was examined at length; fairness in the criminal trial was highlighted as part of the courts' "untrammeled way [which] lies at the foundation of our system of government."[53] A fair example is found in United States v. Atisha,[54] where the U.S. Attorney maintained an "open file" policy permitting defense counsel full access to the evidence that the government intended to put forth as well as the theories upon which the government intended to rely. On the second day of trial, however, the prosecutor for the first time expressed his intention to elicit testimony relating to an offense not specifically enumerated in the indictment. The Sixth U.S. Court of Appeals found that the mere fact that a defendant is not made aware of certain evidence until shortly before or at a trial does not mandate a finding that the government violated its "open file" policy, absent evidence that the government had secreted that evidence. The federal appellate court found that (a) there was not an unreasonable delay between the prosecution's discovery of the evidence and its decision to use it at trial; (b) any prejudice suffered by the defendant did not rise to the level of "serious prejudice"; and (c) the trial court did not abuse its discretion in denying defendant's motion for a new trial.[55] In closing, the court opined that the government is not compelled by statute or the U.S. Constitution to disclose evidentiary details or "to explain the legal theories upon which it intends to rely at trial."[56]

5.6 PRESS-MEDIA ACCESS TO THE CRIMINAL COURTROOM

A prime factor in the guarantee of a fair trial to the defendant is press-media access to the criminal courtroom.[57] The New York Appellate Division, 2nd Dept., in Ladone v. Lerner[58] ruled in 1987 that the New York trial court hearing a murder trial was correct in "declining to permit audio-visual coverage": the appellate court pointed out that "after a further hearing at which the media, prosecution and defense counsel were present" the trial court had cited "seven areas of concern raised by defense counsel,[59] including the Sixth Amendment (the right to a fair trial), but "there must be a sensible accommodation between the First Amendment rights and Sixth Amendment rights." The court observed that the New York legislature, in enacting the law permitting press-media coverage of criminal trials,[60] had recognized that "an enhanced public understanding of the judicial system is not important in maintaining a high level of public confidence in the judiciary," and that criminal proceedings "are complex, often involving human factors that are difficult to measure," and moreover that there "may be inherent problems in court proceeding which could possibly be complicated by audio-visual coverage"; furthermore, "the dignity and decorum of the courtroom" should not be interfered with so as to create "an atmosphere unsuited to calm deliberation and impartial decision making."[61]

Accessibility of the press-media to the criminal courtroom is, however, authorized in twenty-three states that permanently permit cameras in trial courts, and seven additional states have tentatively approved TV coverage of criminal trials. As of 1988 about forty-five states have allowed some form of TV coverage in either criminal trial or appellate proceedings.[62]

It should be noted that the Sixth Amendment right to a fair trial is for the benefit of the defendant alone, as spelled out by the U.S. Supreme Court in Gannett Co. v. DePasquale.[63] This right to a fair (and public) trial can be waived by the defendant with the agreement of the prosecution and the court;[64] but there is no absolute right for members of the public to attend criminal trials under the Sixth and the Fourteenth Amendments.[65] The following year in Richmond Newspapers Co. v. Virginia[66] the highest court ruled that the government cannot limit the stock of information from which members of the public may draw by arbitrarily closing the criminal courtroom doors to the public and to the press-media.[67] In 1982 in Globe Newspaper Co. v. Superior Court[68] the same court reaffirmed its commitment to press-media access to the criminal courtroom by striking down a Massachusetts statute that would have closed trials to the press-media during the testimony of minor victims of sex crimes. In 1984 in Press-Enterprise Co. v. Superior Court[69] the highest court stated that a California judge's order closing the individual voir dire proceedings during the impaneling of the jury in a criminal trial violated constitutional rights, even though the defendant's right to a fair trial was a compelling interest.[70] (The Court ruled that the defendant's right to a fair trial was not protected by the judge's order.) Two years later in 1986 the same parties[71] were again before the U.S. Supreme Court, which then ruled that the California statute giving judges discretion to exclude the public from criminal probable cause hearing violated the First Amendment; the right of access of the press-media includes access to preliminary hearings.[72] It is unfortunate that the highest court here had not the opportunity (nor perhaps the inclination) to consider more fully the criminal defendant's right to a fair trial under the Sixth Amendment.

5.7 THE INDIGENT CRIMINAL DEFENDANT

Fairness and the right of the criminal defendant to a fair trial can also be illustrated by reference to the protection afforded the indigent criminal defendant. Justice Frankfurter in Griffin v. Illinois[73] had opined: "In criminal trials a State can no more discriminate on account of poverty than on account of religion, race, or color. Plainly the ability to pay costs in advance bears no rational relationship to a defendant's guilt or innocence and could not be used as an excuse to deprive a defendant of a fair trial." He continued:

Although a State is not required by the federal Constitution to provide appellate courts or a right to appellate review at all, a State that does grant appellate review cannot do so in a way that discriminates against some convicted defendants on account of their poverty. All States now provide some method of appeal from criminal convictions, recognizing the importance of appellate review to a correct adjudication of guilt or innocence. Statistics show that a substantial proportion of criminal convictions are reversed by state appellate courts. Thus, to deny adequate review to the poor means that many of them may lose their life, liberty, or property because of unjust convictions which appellate courts would overturn. There can be no equal justice where the kind of a trial depends on the amount of money he has. Destitute defendants must be afforded appellate review as defendants who have money enough. . . . [74]

In effect, the due process and equal protection clauses of the Fourteenth Amendment mandated that all indigent criminal defendants be furnished a transcript, for example, at least where allegations that manifest errors occurred at trial are not denied.

A state cannot require an indigent criminal defendant to pay a filing fee before permitting him to appeal his conviction;[75] an indigent must be furnished gratis a transcript of a habeas corpus hearing for his use on appeal from the denial of habeas corpus,[76] and in Mayer v. Chicago[77] the unanimous Court held that an indigent criminal defendant "cannot be denied a record of sufficient completeness to permit proper consideration of his claims" simply because he was convicted of ordinance violations punishable by fine only.[78] In Douglas v. California[79] Justice Douglas found "an unconstitutional line . . . between rich and poor." The instant case showed that the discrimination was not only between "possibly good and obviously bad cases" but between cases where the rich man can require the court to listen to argument of counsel before deciding on the merits, but the poor man cannot. There is lacking, according to Justice Douglas, that equality demanded by the Fourteenth Amendment.[80] In Ross v. Moffit[81] the highest court opined that the indigent defendant must not be denied meaningful access to the judicial system because of poverty, but "the fact that an appeal has been provided does not automatically mean that a State then acts unfairly by refusing to provide counsel to indigent defendants at each stage of the way. Unfairness results only if indigents are singled out by the State and denied" access to the courts.[82] Fair trial for the criminal defendant who is indigent necessitates monetary considerations (for his day in court) from the federal or state governments so that the indigent can fully enjoy his right to a fair trial.

In considering the indigent criminal defendant, a brief word is in order with respect to the right of victims of crime; virtually every State has in recent years enacted some type of victim's rights legislation, although the statutory provisions vary considerably. It would appear that all States, except Hawaii, give victims the right to submit information about the impact of the crime, and about fourteen States give victims the right to be consulted before acceptance of a plea bargain from the criminal defendant. About twenty States give victims the right to speak at sentence hearings of the criminal defendant, and about thirty States give victims the right to notice of the outcome of the criminal proceedings.

NOTES

1. See Rule 11(a) FRCP.
2. See generally United States v. Robertson, 698 F2d 703 (5th Cir., 1983).
3. See Rule 11 of FRCP.
4. See 18 USC 4244 (1982) with respect to competency of defendant to stand trial.
5. See Rule 11(b) of FRCP.
6. See United States v. Bessemer & L. E. Railroad Co., 717 F2d 593 (DC Cir., 1983).
7. See Section and Chapter 7 herein; also see State of North Carolina v. Alford, 400 US 25 (1970).
8. See, for example, Fisher v. Wainright.
9. See Boykin v. Alabama, 395 US 238 (1969).
10. Infra note 2.
11. See United States v. Stalder, 696 F2d 59 (8th Cir., 1982).
12. See Roach v. Martin, 757 F2d 1463 (4th Cir., 1985), cert den 106 S Ct 185 (1985).
13. Infra note 4.
14. 738 F2d 246 (8th Cir., 1984), cert den 105 S Ct 339 (1984).
15. Infra note 12.
16. 718 F2d 277 (8th Cir., 1983), cert den 465 US 1036 (1984).
17. _____NY2d_____, _____NE2d_____ (Nov. 24, 1987).
18. _____NY2d_____, _____NE2d_____ (Nov. 24, 1987).
19. See Section 710.30(3) of CPL.
20.

The People argue in support of an affirmance that the lack of communication between Officer Nash and the Assistant District Attorney is a sufficient excuse under the statute for their noncompliance and that, accordingly, Supreme Court properly allowed them to serve a late notice. In the alternative, they ask us to adopt the reasoning of the Appellate Division that the goal of CPL 710.30 is simply to allow a defendant adequate opportunity to prepare a challenge to the voluntariness of the statement and consequently, if the prosecution's noncompliance does not compromise that objective—that is, if the defendant is not prejudiced by the delay in receiving notice—then the People should not be precluded from using the statement, notwithstanding their lack of "good cause." Finally, the People contend that, if it was error to allow the statement to be used at trial, such error was harmless.

Defendant, on the other hand, urges that the excuse proffered by the People is indistinguishable in principle from the one advanced by the People and rejected by this Court in *People v. Spruill* (47 N.Y. 2d 869). Defendant further argues that good cause is, under the plain terms of the statute, an indispensable requirement, without which permission to file a late notice may not be granted. She asks us to reject the "no prejudice" rule applied by the Appellate Division. Accordingly, she contends that it was error to permit the People to use the statement at trial and that such error was not harmless.

For the reasons that follow, we agree with the defendant's contentions. The order of the Appellate Division should be reversed and a new trial ordered.

21. According to the court, the State of New York argued that the delay should not be excused because "it resulted in no harm to the defendant. . . ."

they contend, the purpose of the statute, which they identify as "giv[ing] a defendant adequate time to prepare his case for questioning the voluntariness of a confession or an admission" (*People v. Briggs, supra*, at 322–323), has not been frustrated because the defendant was not prejudiced by the delay. This position finds support in a number of decisions in the lower courts, especially after the 1976 amendment to CPL 710.30, which accelerated the time for serving notice from "before trial" to "within fifteen days after arraignment" (L. 1976, ch. 194, §3). These decisions (*see, e.g., People v. Swanton*, 107 A.D. 2d 829; *People v. Taylor*, 102 A.D. 2d 944, *aff'd on other grounds* 65 N.Y.2d1; *People v. Brown*, 83 A.D. 2d 699; *People v. Anderson*, 80 A.D. 2d 33) evince an understandable reluctance to deprive the People of useful evidence for failure to comply with a stringent statutory requirement, especially where defendant is not harmed by the omission. Although we fully understand the sentiment, we believe that these decisions conflict with the plain language of the statute, which reflects a legislative policy determination with which the courts may not interfere.

The language which triggers the People's opportunity to serve a late notice—"[f]or good cause shown . . . the court may permit the people to serve such notice"—was unaffected by the 1976 amendment and thus remains an "unqualifie[d] command" that the court may permit service of an untimely notice "only upon a showing of good cause" (*People v. Briggs, supra*, at 323). Such a showing is, therefore, indispensable. Only if that threshold is crossed may the court move on to considerations of prejudice to the defendant, and only then because the existence of prejudice may preclude granting the relief sought by the People, notwithstanding their showing of good cause (*see, People v. Briggs, supra*, at 323); *see also People v. Wright*, 127 Misc. 2d 885, 892; *cf. People v. Basilicato*, 64 N.Y. 2d 103, 117 [construing CPL 700.70]).

That the People have only fifteen days after arraignment to comply does not change the plain meaning of the statutory language. In fact, retention of the good cause requirement in the face of the 1976 amendment reinforces our conclusion that lack of prejudice to the defendant is not a substitute for a demonstration of good cause. Under normal circumstances, the defendant could easily be given an adequate opportunity to challenge the voluntariness of the statement at any time before trial. Thus, acceptance of the argument advanced by the People would require that permission to serve late notices be granted routinely. Such an approach would effectively abrogate the fifteen-day requirement and invite a return to the practice of giving notice at a much later date, even on the eve of trial. Such a result was not the Legislature's intention.

22. 378 US 368 (1965).
23.

It was this version of CPL 710.30 that we addressed in *People v. Briggs* (38 N.Y. 2d 319) and *People v. Spruill* (47 N.Y. 2d 869, *supra*), both of which involved attempts by the prosecution to serve notice during trial. In *Briggs*, the only excuse offered by the prosecutor for the failure to serve the notice before trial, as that statute then required, was a "lack of continuity" in the prosecutor's office; the trial prosecutor apparently did not know whether the notice had been served by his office. The trial court permitted the People to serve a late notice and, after a hearing on the voluntariness, admitted statements made by the defendant to a New York City detective. We vacated the resulting conviction and ordered a new trial, holding that "[l]ack of continuity or other office failure does not constitute the 'unusual circumstances' contemplated by the statute" (*People v. Briggs, supra,* at 324).

In *People v. Spruill,* the excuse offered for failure to give pretrial notice was that the police officer to whom the statement was made had not informed the prosecutor of the confession prior to trial. We held that this excuse was inadequate, finding it no different in principle from the excuse we rejected in *Briggs,* and noting that knowledge on the part of the police department must be imputed to the District Attorney's office (*People v. Spruill, supra,* at 870–871).

and

Although the People complain that the price is too high and the requirements of the statute burdensome, we cannot dilute or disregard the requirements in an effort to avoid exacting the price without trespassing on the Legislature's domain and undermining the purposes of the statute.

Thus, we hold that the People, having failed to establish good cause for their noncompliance with the fifteen-day notice requirement, should not have been permitted to serve a late notice. Accordingly it was error to admit evidence of the statement at trial.

We also agree with defendant that the error was not harmless. Aside from defendant's statement, the only evidence connecting her with the crime was the victim's identification, which was weakened by evidence that he initially described his female assailant to the police as an Hispanic, five-feet, four-inches tall, with a medium complexion and a Puerto Rican accent. According to Detective Kelly's arrest report, however, defendant was five-feet, seven-inches tall, light-skinned, of Irish descent, and spoke with no accent. Given the apparent weakness of the victim's identification, the erroneous admission of defendant's statement that she participated in the crime for which she was on trial cannot be deemed harmless.

24. Infra note 17.

25. _____F2d_____ (6th Cir., 1987).

26. FRE 404(b) states: "Evidence of other crimes, wrongs, or acts is not admissible to prove the character of a person in order to show that he acted in conformity therewith. It may, however, be admissible for other purposes, such as proof of motive, opportunity, intent, preparation, plan, knowledge, identity, or absence of mistake or accident."

27. 754 F2d 33 (1st Cir., 1985).

28. 597 F2d 535 (5th Cir., 1979).

29. 390 US 377 (1968).

30. See 94 Harv L Rev 426 (1980) at 426.

31. Id. at 427.

32. Infra note 28.

33. Id. at 545–546.

34. 618 F2d 1169 (5th Cir., 1980).

35. Id. at 1177.

36. 13 Cal3d 867, 533 P2d 1024 (1975).

37. See generally Trial Magazine (September 1987) at 55 et seq.

38. 106 S Ct 2464 (1986).

39. 55 S Ct 629 (1935) at 633.

40. The ABA Standards for Criminal Justice: The Prosecution Function, Standard 3-5.5, Opening Statement says,

The prosecutor's opening statement should be confined to a brief statement of the issues in the case and to remarks on evidence the prosecutor intends to offer which the prosecutor believes in good faith will be available and admissible. It is unprofessional conduct to allude to any evidence unless there is a good faith and reasonable basis for believing that such evidence will be tendered and admitted in evidence.

Standard 3-5.8, Argument to the Jury, reads as follows:

(a) The prosecutor may argue all reasonable inferences from evidence in the record. It is unprofessional conduct for the prosecutor intentionally to misstate the evidence or mislead the jury as to the inferences it may draw.

(b) It is unprofessional conduct for the prosecutor to express his or her personal belief or opinion as to the truth or falsity of any testimony or evidence of the guilt of the defendant.

(c) The prosecutor should not use arguments calculated to inflame the passions or prejudices of the jury.

(d) The prosecutor should refrain from argument which would divert the jury from its duty to decide the case on the evidence, by injecting issues broader than the guilt or innocence of the accused under the controlling law, or by making predictions of the consequences of the jury's verdict.

(e) It is the responsibility of the court to ensure that final argument to the jury is kept within proper, accepted bounds.

41. National District Attorneys Association, National Prosecution Standards, Standard 17.5, Opening Statements, provides,

A. The prosecutor should be afforded the opportunity to give an opening statement for the purpose of explaining the issues before the court and the procedures of the particular trial.
B. The prosecutor should not allude to any evidence unless there is a good faith and reasonable basis for believing that such evidence will be tendered and admitted into evidence at the trial.

NDAA Standard 17.17, Closing Arguments, reads,

A. Counsel's closing argument to the jury should be characterized by fairness, accuracy, rationality, and a reliance upon the evidence.
B. Because the prosecution bears the burden of proof, the prosecution should have the opportunity to open argument and to rebut the defense's closing argument with the order of the closing statements being prosecution, defense, and prosecution again.
C. Counsel should have the discretion to comment upon the substantive law relevant to the case.
D. The prosecution should have the discretion to comment upon the defense's failure to call witness under its control and favorable to its cause, excluding the defendant, when a name has been raised in opening statements or where defense has introduced the name or existence of an individual, the prosecutor should have the discretion to comment upon the defense's failure to call that witness.

42. Note Rule 3.8 and Rule 8.4 in particular.
43. 468 So2d 978 (Fla., 1985).
44. Id. at 981.
45. 470 NE2d 883 (Ohio, 1984).
46. See ABA Standard 3-5.8(c), infra note 40, and also NDAA Standard 17.17, infra note 41.
47. 295 US 78 (1935).
48. Id. at 88.
49. _____AD2d_____, _____NYS2d_____ (May 18, 1987).
50.

[A] realistic comparison of the lost evidence with the other evidence in this case demonstrates that the imposition of the sanction of dismissal is not required. The impact of the lost rifle, casings and police reports was minimal, as there was no true dispute as to how the crime occurred. Also, the main prosecution witnesses were extensively and effectively cross-examined with respect to the missing evidence. With regard to the lost transcript of the defendant's statement to an Assistant District Attorney after his arrest, we are persuaded that the loss of this statement did not deprive the defendant of a fair trial. First, there was no deliberate suppression of the statement, inasmuch as the prosecutor was not even aware that a statement had been made until the detective revealed it at the *Mapp-Huntley* hearing. Second, the loss of the statement effectively prevented the introduction by the prosecution of evidence concerning it at the trial and, in addition, the entire subject of missing reports provided defense counsel with a basis for cross-examination and for comment in summation on the absence of such reports. In fact, defense counsel made the direct statement to the jury that his client was not receiving a fair trial because of the unavailability of the evidence in question. We thus conclude that the jury was aware of the destruction of the evidence in question and could therefore take this knowledge into account in assessing the strength of the People's case (see, *United States v. Miranda*, 526 F 2d 1319, 1324, 1328, *cert denied* 429 US 821).

51.

Turning briefly to certain other arguments advanced by the defendant on appeal, we conclude that the defendant's guilt was established beyond a reasonable doubt. While there was conflicting psychiatric testimony as to defendant's sanity at the time of the homicide, the resolution of these conflicting expert opinions was a matter for the jury and, absent a serious flaw in the opinion testimony of the People's expert psychiatrist, which we do not find, the jury's finding of sanity should be left undisturbed (see, *People v. Jandell*, 118 AD 2d 656).

The sentence of life imprisonment imposed was not illegal (see, *People v. Pepples*, 32 AD 2d 1041, *affd* 27 NY 2d 785).

We have reviewed the defendant's remaining contentions and find them to be without merit.

52. 370 US 375 (1962).

53. 804 F2d 920 (6th cir., 1986).

54. On fair trial, due process and prosecutorial behavior, see People v. Wheeler, 583 P.2d 748 (Cal. 1978); Commonwealth v. Soares, 387 N.E.2d 499 (Pa. 1979); State v. Gilmore, 511 A.2d 1150 (N.J., 1986); State v. Crespin, 612 P.2d 716 (N.M. App. 1983); Holley v. J.S. Sweeping Co., 192 Cal. Rptr. 74 (Cal. Appl 1983); Oshrin v. Coulter, 688 P.2d 1001 (Ariz. 1985); In re Bower, 700 P.2d 1296 (Cal. 1985) (state based standard for prosecutorial vindictiveness); State v. Glosson, 462 So. 2d 1082 (Fla. 1985); State v. Tuttle, 713 P.2d 703 (Utah 1985); State v. Graves, 700 P.2d 244 (Or. 1985) (statute impermissibly vague).

55. Infra note 53 at 924, citing United States v. Gabriel, 715 F2d 1445 (10th Cir., 1983).

56.

While courts have continuously had the authority and power to maintain order in their courtrooms and to assure litigants a fair trial, the exercise of that bare contempt power is not what is questioned in this case. Here it is asserted that the exercise of the contempt power, to commit a person to jail for an utterance out of the presence of the court, has abridged the accused's liberty of free expression. In this situation the burden upon this Court is to define the limitations upon the contempt power according to the terms of the Federal Constitution.

57. See Warren Freedman, *Press-Media Access to the Criminal Courtroom* (Quorum Books, 1988).

58. _____AD2d_____, _____NYS2d_____ (December 9, 1987). Note the line-up of counsel for the eleven parties to the suit:

Ronald Rubinstein, Kew Gardens, N.Y., for petitioner Ladone.
Bryan Levinson, Kew Gardens, N.Y., for petitioner Lester.
Gabriel B. Leone, Jackson Heights, N.Y., for petitioner Kern.
Stephen G. Murphy, Glendale, N.Y., for petitioner Pirone.
Robert Abrams, Attorney-General, New York, N.Y. (Frederic L. Lieberman of counsel), for respondent.
Rogers & Wells, New York, N.Y. (Richard N. Winfield of counsel), for media intervenors Associated Press and Newsday Press Pool.
Roberta R. Brackman, New York, N.Y., for media intervenors WNBC-TV and the New York Broadcasters' Courtroom Pool.
Squadron, Ellenoff, Plesent & Lehrer, New York, N.Y. (Slade R. Metcalf of counsel), for media intervenor News American Publishers, Inc.
Charles J. Hynes, Deputy Attorney-General, New York, N.Y. (Helman R. Brook of counsel), Special Prosecutor *pro se*.

59.

1. Although the First Amendment (freedom of the press and the public's right to know) is not an issue here, the Sixth Amendment (right to a fair trial) is an issue here. The media in all its forms (with the exception of cameras) has covered the trial extensively and responsibly. The presence of cameras in the courtroom at this stage of the proceeding cannot add any more, but may affect the rights of the defendants. There must be a sensible accommodation between the First Amendment rights and Sixth Amendment rights.

2. The timing of the implementation of the cameras is objectionable in the final stages of the proceeding. During the selection of the jury, it was never predicated there was a possibility that there would be audiovisual coverage of this trial. There should have been maximum opportunity to prepare the jury for the introduction of cameras in the courtroom and to access the reaction of the prospective jurors so that counsel could intelligently exercise their peremptory challenges. It is too late to ask the jury what effect the cameras will have on their deliberations and their ultimate decision—the guilt or innocence of the defendants.

3. This is an experimental program and it mandates a pre-trial conference. There was no pre-trial conference here, to the detriment of the defendants.

4. There will be a psychological effect on the jury which is difficult to assess. The effect could change the balance of the trial and it is too dangerous. In the event of a conviction, defense has no remedy as defense is not permitted to inquire into jury verdicts and whether or not the cameras affected their deliberations.

5. The jury has sat over two months with the presence of the media throughout the entire proceedings. They are relaxed and comfortable. It is unfair to this jury to now advise them about cameras in the courtroom. They have no input into whether cameras

should be in the courtroom. It is unfair to them and it is presumptious to say that it will not affect them.

6. Jurors were never consulted during the voir dire. There were a number of jurors who felt uncomfortable by the presence of the media and they were excused. More jurors might have been excused had the defense known what effect cameras would have on them.

7. The spectators at this trial have resulted in a very charged audience. The defense does not want to be restricted to their summations in the fear that what they say may trigger off demonstrations or disturbances in the courtroom by the presence of cameras.

60. New York Laws of 1987, Chapter 113.

61. Id. at Section 1 thereof.

62. See NLJ (December 21, 1987) at 13 et seq.

63. 443 US 368 (1979).

64. Id. at 384.

65. Id. at 391.

66. 448 US 555 (1980).

67. See generally 19 Conn L Rev 561 (1987).

68. 457 US 596 (1982).

69. 464 US 501 (1984).

70. Id. at 510.

71. 106 S Ct 2735 (1986).

72. Infra note 64 at 578.

73. 351 US 12 (1956).

74. Id. Also see 25 U Chi L Rev 151 (1957).

75. See Burns v. Ohio, 360 US 252 (1959).

76. See Long v. District Court, 385 US 192 (1966).

77. 404 US 189 (1971).

78. ''The size of the defendant's pocketbook bears no more relationship to his guilt or innocence in a non-felony than in a felony case.'' Nor can it be argued that appellant's interest in a transcript in a case where he is not subject to imprisonment is outweighed by the state's fiscal and other interests in not burdening the appellate process: ''*Griffin* does not represent a balance between the needs of the accused and the interests of society; its principle is a flat prohibition against pricing indigent defendants out of as effective an appeal as would be available to others able to pay their own way.''

79. 372 US 353 (1963).

80.

There is lacking that equality demanded by the Fourteenth Amendment where the rich man, who appeals as of right, enjoys the benefit of counsel's examination into the record, research of the law, and marshalling of arguments on his behalf, while the indigent, already burdened by a preliminary determination that his case is without merit, is forced to shift for himself. The indigent, where the record is unclear or the errors are hidden, has only the right to a meaningless ritual, while the rich man has a meaningful appeal.

The pessimism of the dissent of Justice Clark is evident:

[In *Griffin*] we took pains to point out that the State was free to "find other means of affording adequate and effective appellate review to indigent defendants." Here California has done just that in its procedure for furnishing attorneys for indigents on appeal. We all know that the overwhelming percentage of in forma pauperis appeals are frivolous. [California's courts] after examining the record certified that [appointment of counsel] would be neither advantageous to the petitioners nor helpful to the court. It, therefore, refused to go throught the useless gesture of appointing an attorney. In my view neither the Equal Protection Clause nor the Due Process Clause requires more. [I]f the Court is correct it may be that we should first clean up our own house. We have afforded indigent litigants much less protection than has California. Last Term we received over 1,200 in forma pauperis applications in none of which had we appointed attorneys or required a record. Some were appeals of right. Still we denied the petitions or dismissed the appeals on the moving papers alone. At the same time we had hundreds of paid cases in which we permitted petitions or appeals to be filed with not only records but briefs by counsel, after which they were disposed of in due course. . . . There is an old adage [that] "People who live in glass houses had best not throw stones." I dissent.

81. 417 US 600 (1974).
82. According to the Court,

The suggestion that a State is responsible for providing counsel to one petitioning this Court simply because it initiated the prosecution which led to the judgment sought to be reviewed is unsupported by either reason or authority. It would be quite as logical under the rationale of *Douglas* and *Griffin*, and indeed perhaps more so, to require that the Federal Government or this Court furnish and compensate counsel for petitioners who seek certiorari here to review state judgments of conviction. Yet this Court has followed a consistent policy of denying applications for appointment of counsel by persons seeking to file jurisdictional statements or petitions for certiorari in this Court. In the light of these authorities, it would be odd, indeed, to read the Fourteenth Amendment to impose such a requirement on the States, and we decline to do so.

6

The Role of the Jury in the Speedy and Fair Criminal Trial

6.1 INTRODUCTION

The Sixth Amendment expressly affords criminal defendants the right to trial "by an impartial jury of the State and district wherein the crime shall have been committed, which district shall have been previously ascertained by law." In determining when this right to jury trial attaches,[1] the courts have generally distinguished between serious crimes[2] and petty offenses,[3] the former entitling the defendant to a jury trial and the latter not entitling the defendant to a jury trial in accordance with the common law. In Patton v. United States[4] the U.S. Supreme Court observed that both the Sixth Amendment and Article III, Section 2, Clause 3, of the U.S. Constitution[5] delineate the concept of jury trial, and that both provisions proclaim that "(a) the jury should consist of twelve men, neither more or less; (b) the trial should be in the presence and under the superintendence of a judge having the power to instruct them as to the law and advise them in respect of the facts; and (c) the verdict should be unanimous. . . . "[6] Justice Sutherland opined that the effect of the constitutional provisions in respect of trial by jury was that the criminal defendant had the power

to waive a trial by a constitutional jury and submit to trial by a jury of less than twelve persons, or by the court . . . Trial by jury is the normal, and, with occasional exceptions, the preferable mode of disposing of issues of fact

in criminal cases above the grade of petty offenses. In such cases the value
and appropriateness of jury trial have been established by long experience,
and are not now to be denied. Not only must the right of the accused to a trial
by a constitutional jury be jealously preserved, but the maintenance of the jury
as a fact-finding body in criminal cases is of such importance and has such a
place in our tradition, that, before any waiver can become effective, the consent of the government counsel and the sanction of the court must be had, in
addition to the express and intelligent consent of the defendant.[7]

Historically, the institution of trial by jury had its beginnings in
England more than 800 years ago when the legal mind of King Henry
II remodeled the "sworn inquest" of the Norman conqueror King William I, and "cast it into the mold of the jury."[8] The qualifications of
jurors at common law changed from property ownership[9] to mere residence in the community, whether the juror is male or female.[10]

The criminal defendant's right to a jury trial does not apply in juvenile court proceedings.[11] A defendant may waive his/her right to a
jury trial, provided that the waiver is done voluntarily, knowingly, and
intelligently.[12] Under the Federal Rules of Criminal Procedure any waiver
must be in writing.[13]

6.2 COMPOSITION OF THE JURY AND
CHALLENGES TO JURY PROCEDURE

Historically, juries have been composed of twelve persons,[14] but in
the United States a jury of fewer than twelve persons but more than
five persons has been held to satisfy the requisites of the Sixth Amendment.[15] In Ballew v. Georgia[16] the U.S. Supreme Court ruled that a
five-person jury violated both the Sixth and the Fourteenth Amendments because that small number of jurors would not fully represent
minority members of the community. Rule 23(b) of the Federal Rules
of Criminal Procedure authorizes a waiver of the twelve-person jury if
the agreement is in writing and is approved by the federal district trial
court.[17]

In the federal courts it has been held that a criminal defendant has
a right to a unanimous verdict from the jury.[18] [Section 31(a) of the
Federal Rules of Criminal Procedure states that "the verdict shall be
unanimous."] In the state courts the jurors' vote is much more critical;
in Buren v. Louisiana,[19] for example, a conviction by five members

of a six-person jury was held to violate the criminal defendant's right to a jury trial, while in Apodaca v. Oregon[20] a conviction by ten jurors out of a twelve-person jury was deemed to satisfy the Sixth Amendment's right to a jury trial!

Jury procedures have been challenged over the years, as shown in the 1917 Arizona Supreme Court decision in Babb v. State.[21] Here a newspaper article purported to "relate certain facts of and concerning the commission of the offense charged" was viewed by jurors. The court in granting the defendants a new trial declared: "The law has provided by very strict rules that the jury shall not, after being sworn, receive any evidence outside of the court in the due course of the trial or be subject to any extrajudicial influences or suggestions whatever during the pendency of the case."[22] The Arizona court concluded: "When a juror enters upon the trial of a criminal case, the law contemplates his withdrawal from the public . . . . Perfect impartiality in the juror is the object of the law. Anything not legitimately arising out of the trial of the case, which tends to destroy the impartiality of the juror, should be discountenanced."[23]

Jurors must be drawn from a fair cross-section of the community, or the criminal defendant may successfully argue that his right to an impartial jury is infringed. In Duren v. Missouri,[24] for example, the U.S. Supreme Court ruled that the jury selection system excluding women who requested not to serve on the jury was in violation of the Sixth Amendment. And in United States v. Clark[25] the Seventh U.S. Court of Appeals stated that white defendants have a constitutional and a statutory right to be tried by a jury from which black persons have not been systematically excluded. Where jurors are selected in an intentionally discriminatory manner, the equal protection clause of the Fourteenth Amendment provides an additional basis for challenging the composition of the jury.[26] Due process of law under the Fourteenth Amendment may be offended by the jury selection system, as shown in Anderson v. Frey[27] where bystander jurors were selected by sheriff's subordinates; in contrast, see Hobby v. United States[28] wherein the highest court found that the discrimination in the selection of the grand jury chairperson did not threaten the interests of the criminal defendant.

The Jury Selection and Service Act of 1968[29] established statutory guidelines for selecting juries in the federal courts. Random selection from voter lists and exclusion on the basis of objective criteria only,

are described under the Act, which, in effect, constitutes a "codifica-
tion" of the Sixth Amendment postulate on the impartial jury.

A corollary issue concerns the disclosure of juror names and addresses, and the New York Court of Appeals in Matter of Newsday,
Inc. v. Size[30] on December 23, 1987, opined that a daily newspaper
was not entitled to such information, even under the State Freedom of
Information Law. According to the court,

It is this state's policy to provide all litigants with the right to trial by a jury
randomly selected from a fair cross-section of the community. In order to
achieve this goal, Judiciary Law article 16 creates a detailed procedure for
selection of jurors which requires, among other things, that the commissioner
of jurors be made privy to details of jurors' personal lives obtained through
the juror qualification questionnaires (see, Judiciary Law §§509(a), 513; *People v. Guzman*, 60 NY2d 403, 414–415). Recognizing that many prospective
jurors would be averse to having these details made public and that disclosures
could result in harassment of jurors or attempts at retribution or intimidation,
the Legislature has provided that the questionnaires be kept confidential and
exempt from disclosure except upon an application made pursuant to Judiciary
Law §509(a).

While Judiciary Law §509(a) refers only to the juror qualification questionnaires, its obvious purpose is to provide a cloak of confidentiality for the
information which the questionnaires contain. It is the knowledge about the
jurors—the private details obtained from the questionnaires concerning their
spouses' names, the names and ages of their children, their home telephone
numbers, occupations, educational backgrounds, and criminal records, if any—
which the statute is designed to protect from public disclosure (see, *Matter of
Herald Co. v. Roy*, 107 AD2d 515, 520; see also, *People v. Perkins*, 125
AD2d 816, 817–818). Petitioner's interpretation—that the statute exempts from
disclosure only the actual questionnaires—could not have been intended. It is
the information from the questionnaires, not the forms themselves which, if
made public, could invade the jurors' privacy interests or threaten their safety
and that information, therefore, was made confidential. Because petititioner's
proposed construction would defeat the very purpose of the statute and render
it ineffective it must be rejected (*see*, McKinney's Statutes, §§92, 96, 144).
We hold, then, that Judiciary Law §509(a) shields from disclosure not only
the juror qualification questionnaires but also those portions of other records
containing information obtained from the questionnaires.

and

Finally, petitioner argues that because the names and addresses have already been made public during *voir dire*, granting their release in this petition could result in no further invasion of their privacy interests. From the record, however, it clearly appears that, in voir dire, the home addresses of the jurors were not disclosed—only the general area where they lived (see also, *Matter of Herald Co. v. Roy*, 107 AD2d 515, 518, *supra*). Moreover, that some of the information sought may have been orally revealed during the jury selection process, cannot alter the effect of Judiciary Law §509(a) in categorically prohibiting the public disclosure of any records containing information obtained from the juror questionnaires.

6.3 THE VOIR DIRE

The criminal defendant, in order to secure his right to a fair trial and an impartial jury under the Sixth Amendment, is entitled to evaluate the caliber of the prospective juror through voir dire examination. The trial court is also in position to conduct the voir dire examination.[31] The thrust of the voir dire is to ferret out prejudice or bias which can interfere with the fair trial right of the criminal defendant. The party requesting specific voir dire questioning has the burden of showing a reasonable possibility of prejudice, unless the case itself involves clearly racial overtones, or known community prejudices, or bias or distorting influences among the jurors.[32] Appellate courts will readily reverse where the improperly conducted voir dire resulted in an unfair trial.[33] The trial court may exclude, for cause, any prospective juror whose voir dire responses indicate potentiality for prejudice or bias or inability to render an impartial judgment.[34] The criminal defendant may also challenge prospective jurors for lack of competence to serve on the jury.[35] The right to peremptory challenges is essential to a fair trial and may not be impaired;[36] note that the Federal Rules of Criminal Procedure expressly limits the number of peremptory challenges that the parties may make, although the trial court can add to that number of peremptory challenges where warranted.[37] Above all, the Sixth Amendment does provide the criminal defendant with a right to a panel of impartial jurors, and it is up to the trial court to ensure that juror impartiality is granted and is maintained throughout the trial.[38]

Selection of jurors is time-consuming and expensive; it is generally felt that examination of the panel by the court does produce the best results in certain jurisdictions. A strong trial judge, with secure tenure, is able to withstand the urgency of defense and prosecuting counsel to obtain advantages in the composition of the jury.

The peremptory challenge to jurors has no constitutional basis;[39] it is nevertheless one of the most important rights secured by the criminal accused.[40] Any restraint upon the exercise of that right of peremptory challenges will be condemned by appellate courts. There are generally two methods of exercising peremptory challenges, the sequential method and the struck-jury method.[41] The former method involves the exercise of challenges for cause and peremptory challenges *prior* to the examination of all potential jurors; each juror is treated individually.[42] The struck-jury method delays the exercise of peremptory challenges until *after* all eligible jurors are questioned; the number of potential jurors examined equals the sum of the jury size plus the total number of peremptory challenges available to both parties along with any necessary challenges for cause. The sequential method requires that attorneys make decisions on the exercise of their peremptory challenges under a condition of fundamental uncertainty; they do not know who will replace those jurors who are challenged. There is significant less uncertainty in the struck-jury method, which is deemed to be superior for the intelligent exercise of peremptory challenges; this method allows for the gathering of information on all potential jurors before any peremptory challenges are exercised.[43]

Peremptory challenges have their origins in the English common law, and were ingrained in the essence of judicial procedure. The first U.S. Congress observed the defendant's right of peremptory challenges as early as 1790.[44] In Swaine v. Alabama[45] the highest Court traced the history of peremptory challenges and acknowledged the possibility for discrimination in the proceedings, "Jury . . . should be selected as individuals for discrimination on the basis of individual qualifications and not as members of a race."[46] Twenty-one years later in Boston v. Kentucky[47] the Court overruled the Swaine case and established a bipartite test with which the validity of peremptory challenges could be attacked. While there is no constitutional right to balanced composition of the jury, the Equal Protection Clause prohibits the challenge of potential jurors solely on the basis of race. The party being challenged must show that "a permissible racially neutral selection criteria and procedure have produced the monochromatic result." The U.S. Supreme Court here in 1985 determined that discrimination could not be tolerated by either the prosecution or the defense counsel.

A New York case, People v. Scott[48] is illustrative: here the Negress prostitute was convicted of murder and grand larceny of a white, retired police officer; during the voir dire all five potential Negro jurors were excused by the prosecution using peremptory challenges. The New York Court of Appeals held that the defendant established a prime facie case of racial discrimination during the jury selection in that the blacks were a heterogeneous group which included different sexes, occupations, and diverse social backgrounds. The Court reversed the conviction and ordered a new trial.

The relatively new concept of the "anonymous jury"[49] was coined in 1979 by Judge Henry F. Werker of the U.S. District Court for the Southern District of New York in the United States v. Barnes.[50] Here the trial judge, on his own inititative, ordered that the jurors remain "anonymous" because of the nature of the criminal acts alleged. The identities and addresses of each of the jurors was kept secret from the parties to the criminal proceeding; jurors were known by their numbers, and during the voir dire the prospective jurors were asked questions that could not identify their residence or job site or their names. Judge Werker refused here to inquire into the ethnicity or race of the jurors. On appeal, the Second U.S. Court of Appeals[51] affirmed the convictions, holding that the jury selection process was a proper response to the "sordid history" of narcotics in New York city. The federal appellate court concluded that neither statutory nor constitutional requisites made mandatory the disclosure of information about the jurors unrelated to any issues as to which prejudice may prevent an impartial verdict by an impartial jury. Jurors have no obligation to disclose their identities publicly and take responsibility for their decisions. The criminal defendants' substantive rights under the Sixth Amendment were protected because defense counsel had full opportunity of examination.[52] In United States v. Rosado[53] a non-narcotics case, the request for the anonymous jury was granted because the case involved violence allegedly to achieve political independence. Later in United States v. Thomas[54] the Second U.S. Court of Appeals observed that "as a practical matter, we cannot expect jurors to take the chances on what might happen to them as a result of a guilty verdict." In effect, the anonymous jurors were entitled to protection not just from retaliation by the defendants but also from fear of retaliation. In United

States v. Persico[55] the federal district court, in finding a need for an anonymous jury, stated that the court must look to the following factors:

(i) whether defendants are alleged to have engaged in dangerous and unscrupulous conduct, with particular consideration of whether such conduct was part of a large-scale organized criminal enterprise; (ii) whether defendants have engaged in past attempts to interfere with the judicial process, and (iii) whether there has been a substantial degree of pre-trial publicity such as to enhance the possibility that jurors' names would become public and thus expose them to intimidation by defendants' friends or enemies or harassment by the public.

6.4 THE JURY AND OBSTRUCTION OF JUSTICE

The criminal defendant is entitled to the impartial jury and the fair trial, which means tht the jury must be unprejudiced by extraneous influences. In Remmer v. United States[56] the U.S. Supreme Court ruled that any private communication, contact, or tampering with jurors during the criminal trial was presumptively prejudicial, obstructive of justice, and in violation of the rights of the criminal defendant. Prejudice is presumed when the conduct is made without the full knowledge of all the parties and not in accordance with judicial instructions or court rules.[57] But mere speculation does not trigger a court's duty to investigate; that duty arises when the party alleging jury misconduct in jury decision-making makes a showing of extrinsic influence sufficient to overcome the presumption of jury impartiality. Unauthorized documents (police interviews and transcripts of other court proceedings) in the jury-deliberation room prompted a mistrial in United States v. Mackay.[58] The Alaskan trial court here had interviewed jurors for five hours, finding that seven jurors had read part or all of the material, and therefore were interfered with in their decision-making functions. In such situation where material has found its way into the jury room the court must determine whether such material has influenced a verdict by examining the nature of the material, the manner in which it was conveyed, and the extent to which jurors considered it in reaching their decision.[59]

In the federal courts the statute on obstruction of justice[60] includes a number of different and separate offenses; Section 1505, for example, provides that "whoever corruptly . . . influences, obstructs, or impedes or endeavors to influence, obstruct, or impede the due and proper administration of the law under which any pending proceeding is being had before any department or agency of the United States . . . shall be fined not more than $5,000 or imprisoned for not more than 5 years, or both.'' Section 1505 covers jury tampering as well as falsification, alteration, destruction, and concealment of incriminating documents and records,[61] all perhaps redounding to the detriment of the criminal defendant in a particular situation.

6.5 PRE-TRIAL AND TRIAL PUBLICITY

The jury is frequently the unwilling victim of pre-trial and trial publicity, but it is the criminal defendant whose right to a fair trial by an impartial jury that is endangered.[62] In Williams v. Griswald[63] the Eleventh U.S. Court of Appeals found a ''media circus'' during pre-trial and trial times that could only constitute presumptive prejudicial publicity. In Patton v. Yount[64] the U.S. Supreme Court overturned the trial court's finding of impartiality upon finding manifest error, although adverse pre-trial publicity could have created a presumption of prejudice and could have rendered a juror's claim of impartiality incredible. Earlier the Court, however, in Nebraska Press Association v. Stuart[65] had ruled that pervasive adverse publicity did not necessarily lead to an unfair trial, because the tone and extent of publicity influencing a jury's capacity for fair decision-making can be shaped by the trial judge, counsel for both sides, police, and other court officials.

In Sheppard v. Maxwell[66] the highest court had observed that, while there is a ''reasonable likelihood that prejudicial news prior to trial will prevent a fair trial'' for the criminal defendant, the trial judge should still continue with the proceeding until the threat abates, or the trial judge should transfer the proceeding to another jurisdiction where publicity about the case is less pervasive. Indeed, a change of venue may be the answer to assure impartiality when no other effort by the trial judge will ensure fairness at trial.[67] Section 21(a) of the Federal Rules of Criminal Procedure so provides for transfer of criminal cases:

The court upon motion of the defendant shall transfer the proceeding as to him to another district whether or not such district is specified in the defendant's motion if the court is satisfied that there exists in the district where the prosecution is pending, so great a prejudice against the defendant that he cannot obtain a fair and impartial trial at any place fixed by law for holding court in that district.

The U.S. Supreme Court in the Sheppard case[68] listed several steps that a trial court might take "to reduce the appearance of prejudicial material and to protect the jury from outside influence,"[69] to wit: limiting the number of reporters in the courtroom; regulating the conduct of reporters in the courtroom; insulating witnesses from exposure to the press-media; controlling the release of information by police officers, witnesses, parties and their counsel; prohibiting extrajudicial statements which would divulge prejudicial matters by any attorney, party, witness or court official; and warning the press-media of the impropriety of publishing or broadcasting material not introduced in evidence at the trial.[70]

6.6 THE SEVENTH AMENDMENT AND THE CIVIL JURY

The Seventh Amendment to the U.S. Constitution preserves the jury trial in *civil* cases, and "no fact tried by a jury shall be otherwise reexamined in any Court of the United States, than according to the rules of the common law." But this somewhat ambiguous language requires a court to interpret the Seventh Amendment by resort to "the appropriate rules of the common law established at the time of the adoption of that constitutional provision in 1791."[71] In Ross v. Bernhard[72] the highest court ruled that a civil jury trial was required for a shareholder's derivative action in federal courts.[73] In Colgrove v. Battin[74] the Court determined that it was constitutionally permissible to allow six-person civil juries. As the court in Galloway v. United States[75] expressed it, the Seventh Amendment "was designed to preserve the basic institution of jury trial in only its most fundamental elements, not the great mass of procedural forms and details, varying even then so widely among common law jurisdictions."[76]

Rule 39(c) of the Federal Rules of Civil Procedure provides that "in all actions not triable of right by a jury, the court upon motion or its own initiative may try any issue with an advisory jury. . . . Indeed, the utilization of an advisory jury is a phenomenon that defies comparison with other juries, whether civil or criminal.[77] Since an advisory jury trial is tried formally before the bench, the judge is free to disregard the findings of the advisory jury, which is apparently limited to civil cases.[78] Note that Rule 52(a) states that "in all actions tried upon the facts without a jury or with an advisory jury, the court shall find the facts specially and state separately its conclusions of law thereon." Since one of the reasons for the advisory jury is to encourage and promote community participation in the legal process,[79] advisory juries have particularly been prominent in civil obscenity cases.[80] The U.S. Supreme Court's community-based obscenity standard for constitutional restraints of obscene material has promoted the widespread use of advisory juries.[81]

NOTES

1. See generally 74 Georgetown L J 751 (1986) at 776 et seq.
2. Id. at 777.
3. See Duncan v. Louisiana, 391 US 145 (1968) at 159–161.
4. 281 US 276 (1929).
5. The trial of all crimes, except in cases of impeachment, shall be by jury; and such trial shall be held in the State where the said crimes shall have been committed; but when not committed within any State, the trial shall be at such place or places as Congress may by law have directed."
6.

A constitutional jury means twelve men as though that number had been specifically named; and it follows that when reduced to eleven it ceases to be such a jury quite as effectively as though the number had been reduced to a single person. This conclusion seems self-evident, and no attempt has been made to overthrow it save by what amounts to little more than a suggestion that by reducing the number of the jury to eleven or ten the infraction of the Constitution is slight, and the courts may be trusted to see that the process of reduction shall not be unduly extended. But the constitutional question cannot thus be settled by the simple process of ascertaining that the infraction assailed is unimportant when compared with similar but more serious infractions which might be conceived. To uphold the voluntary reduction of a jury from twelve to eleven upon the ground that the reduction—though, it destroys the jury of the Constitution—is only a slight reduction, is not to interpret that instrument but to disregard it. It is not our province to measure the extent to which the Constitution has been contravened and ignore the violation, if in our opinion, it is not, relatively as bad as it might have been.

7. "And the duty of the trial court in that regard is not to be discharged as a mere matter of rote, but with sound and advised discretion, with an eye to avoid unreasonable or undue departures from that mode of trial or from any of the essential elements thereof, and with a caution increasing in degree as the offenses dealt with increase in gravity."

8. See Hulme, "Our American Heritage of Freedoms from the English Constitution," 32 ABAJ (July 1921) at 849 et seq:

In Roman law the sworn inquest had been cradled. Used in the field of administration it passed into the hands of the Franks, from whom the Normans adopted it. The officials of William the Conqueror put groups of men under oath. From them they obtained the economic facts which composed his Domesday Book. The two immediate successors of William I occasionally employed the sworn inquest to give evidence in civil suits being tried in royal courts. . . .

Soon after his accession in 1154, Henry II began to right the wrongs perpetrated during the last two decades. Justice must rule again, justice emanating from the evidence presented by a man's neighbors under oath. In civil law the King widely extended the use of the sworn inquest. He applied it to possessory actions where twelve men under oath were asked to state from their knowledge which party to a suit had possessed a piece of land at a particular time. He extended it to proprietary actions where the grand assize composed of twelve sworn men chosen by four neighbors decided which of the litigants had a better right to the parcel of land in dispute. In the Assizes of Clarendon and Northampton, King Henry left the civil action juries as legacies to his countrymen and the world.

In these great legal documents Henry II left more to posterity. Convinced that many a criminal was escaping justice because of his power in a community, because an individual was afraid to accuse him, the King hit upon an idea. Let the sheriff appoint twelve or more men of standing from a locality who were to state the opinion of their neighbors that certain men were believed to have committed crimes. The accusing jury, the prototype of the modern grand jury, was born. But the criminal thus accused was still brought before the bar of heaven to make his proof through the ordeals of hot water or hot iron. Henry II was not satisfied; but his ingenious mind could find no substitute. He had laid, however, an ineradicable foundation of the jury system.

That it should continue to develop and thrive was inevitable in an England with a substantial middle class whose interests were being diverted into the channels of local government and royal justice. From that middle class were taken the men who composed the petty or trial jury in criminal cases as it gradually evolved from the accusing and civil action juries during the thirteenth century. Aided by the prohibition of the Church in 1215 whereby the clergy could no longer participate in the ordeals and by stern practices of *peine forte et dure* whereby the accused was forced through torture to put himself upon God and his country, the trial jury slowly took shape.

Instead of being chiefly a body of witnesses and only incidentally judges of fact the trial jury began to place more emphasis on judging facts and less on presenting evidence. The unanimous verdict began to go hand in hand with the voice of the country. Witnesses were being distinguished from jurymen. By the middle of the fourteenth century the essential features of the English trial jury had evolved. But the juryman was still a witness, and a better juryman if he had been a witness. That prevented the trial jury of the fourteenth through the seventeenth centuries from being equated with the jury of today.

It must not be forgotten that in the fifteenth century the jury system nearly foundered on the rock of baronial greed and corruption. It was saved by drastic action on the part of the King's Council and Star Chamber.

By the seventeenth century, when English institutions began to cross the Atlantic ocean, trial by jury was so embedded in the civilization of Englishmen that it was accepted by the colonists in America as part of their heritage from the mother country.

9. See Commonwealth v. Maxwell, 114 A 825 (Penna., 1921):

At an early period it was required that a juror should be possessed of some property as a qualification: Proffat on Jury Trials, section 115. At common law, jurors were required to be freeholders and the qualification continued by statute from the time of Henry V down to that of George II: 20 Amer. Law Register 437. The statute of the 2d Henry V, c. 3, requires jurors that pass upon a man's life to have forty shillings per annum freehold. At the time of the adoption of Pennsylvania's first Constitution in 1776, there was a property qualification in England for all jurors: 3 Blackstone 362. . . .

Summing up, we conclude, (1) there was no absolute and fixed qualification of jurors at common law, and from very ancient times their qualifications were fixed by act of parliament; (2) the qualification of jurors was not the thing spoken of by the section of the Constitution under consideration; (3) the words "as heretofore" in that section refer to the kinds of cases triable before juries and the trial, not the qualifications of the jurors; (4) the designation "qualified elector" embraces all electors at the time jurors are selected from the body of electors; (5) the term "electors" embraces those who may be added to the electorate from time to time.

10. Id. According to the court, "the pending case calls for the immediate decision only of the right of women to serve as jurors. . . . We entertain no doubt, however, that women are eligible to serve as jurors in all the Commonwealth's courts."

11. See McKeiver v. Pennsylvania, 403 US 528 (1971), and note the Youth Corrections Act, 18 USC 5005–5026 (1982).

12. See United States v. Medina-Cervantes, 690 F2d 715 (9th Cir., 1982).

13. Section 23(a) of FR Crim P.

14. Infra note 6.

15. See Williams v. Florida, 399 US 78 (1970).

16. 435 US 223 (1978).

17. See United States v. Stewart, 700 F2d 702 (11th Cir., 1983) as to a larger jury.

18. See Andres v. United States, 333 US 740 (1948).

19. 441 US 130 (1979).

20. 406 US 404 (1972).

21. 163 P 259 (Ariz., 1917).

22.

Notwithstanding these precautions of the law, the jury was permitted to obtain on the last day of the trial, that had lasted six days, a copy of a newspaper, stating that one of the appellants had been guilty of a felony, to wit, embezzlement, and that he was saved from the penitentiary only because he made good on the cast taken. One of the jurors, it is shown, read the article aloud to all the other jurors. It was new matter, foreign to the issue on trial, and could not, by any rule of evidence, have been introduced before the jury. The natural and inevitable result, it would seem, of permitting such a charge to come before the jury without any opportunity to explain it away, even if it had been competent evidence, would be to influence and prejudice the jury against the appellants. They might well have reasoned that if the appellant, Phillips, was a common criminal, the probabilities were that he was guilty of the crime for which he was on trial.

While it is not a commendable practice to permit juries to read from newspapers detailed statements of the evidence when correctly reported, it is not apparent that any prejudice would be created in the minds of the jury against the defendant; therefore courts have uniformly refused to grant new trials by reason thereof. But where a newspaper report has departed from a fair and honest statement of the evidence and has interpolated facts derogatory to the defendant and likely to excite passion and prejudice on the part of the jury against the defendant, the courts, as a general rule, have not hesitated to grant new trials.

23.

It is claimed by the respondent that the jury in this case could not have honestly or intelligently returned any other verdict than the one they did, and therefore this court should affirm the judgment. It is difficult for this court to say what the verdict of the jury might have been if they had been correctly instructed as to the law, or if they had not read the newspaper article complained of. The evidence consists of 800 pages of typewritten matter; we have read it sufficiently to discover that there is great conflict of testimony. We do not feel like assuming the functions of the jury and determining the weight of the testimony especially in view of the palpable misdirection of the jury as to the law and the possible, and indeed probable, prejudice and bias created in the minds of the jury against the appellants by reason of the very damaging statement contained in the newspaper.

Judgment of the lower court is reversed and cause remanded, with the directions that appellants be granted a new trial.

24. 439 US 357 (1979).
25. 737 F2d 679 (7th Cir., 1984).
26. See Swain v. Alabama, 380 US 202 (1965).
27. 715 F2d 1304 (8th Cir., 1983).
28. 104 S Ct 3093 (1984).
29. 28 USC 1861 to 1877 (1982).
30. _____NY2d_____, _____NE2d_____ (December 23, 1987).
31. Note Section 24(a) of FRCP, for example.
32. See United States v. Robinson, 475 F2d 376 (DC Cir., 1973).
33. See United States v. Spaar, 748 F2d 1249 (8th Cir., 1984).
34. Note 28 USC 1866(c)(2) (1982), and see Rogers v. Rulo, 712 F2d 363 (8th Cir., 1983).
35. Cf. United States v. Fuentes-Coba, 738 F2d 1191 (11th Cir., 1984) where defendant expressly passed up his opportunity to have the unqualified juror replaced.

36. Infra note 26.
37. See Section 24(b) of FRCP setting forth twenty challenges for serious crimes, etc.
38. See Sheppard v. Maxwell, 384 US 333 (1966).
39. See Stilson v. United States, 250 US 583, 40 S Ct (1919).
40. Note Pointer v. United States, 151 US 396, 14 S Ct 410 (1894); also see Case & Comment (January–February 1988) at 18 et seq.
41. See G. Bermant, Conduct of the Voir Dire Examination: Practices and Opinions of Federal District Judges (Federal Judicial Center, 1977).
42. Infra note 40 in Case & Comment at 20:

Under the group style of questioning, a panel or group of potential jurors is examined by one of the parties and any challenges are exercised. Any potential jurors removed are replaced by other potential jurors. These replacements are questioned by the examining party and any challenges are exercised. This process continues until the examining party is satisfied with the jury or the party has exhausted his peremptory challenges and no challenges for cause are granted. The jury is then passed over for consideration by the second party who proceeds in the same manner as did the first party. Once the second party is satisfied with the jury, the first party is allowed to question those remaining potential jurors who it had yet to examine. This process of examination and replacement continues until both parties either pass the jury or one or both parties can no longer influence the composition of the jury.

43. See Case & Comment, note 38.2 at 24.
44. Note 44 U of Pitt L Rev 675 (Spring 1983).
45. 380 US 202 (1964).
46. Id. at 204.
47. 476 US 79, 106 S Ct 1712 (1985); see ABAJ (April 1, 1988) at 54 et seq.
48. 70 NY2d 420 (1987) Also note the following recent cases: U.S. v. David, 803 F2d 1567 (11th Cir., 1986); Fleming v. Kemp, 794 F2d 1478 (11th Cir., 1986); Clark v. Bridgeport, 645 F Supp 890 (Conn., 1986); and U.S. v. Ratcliff, 806 F2d 1253 (5th Cir., 1986).
49. See Lewis, "Cost to Justice When the Jury is Anonymous," NLJ (November 2, 1987) at 19 et seq.
50. _____F Supp_____ (SDNY, 1979).
51. 604 F2d 121 (2nd Cir., 1979).
52. Note that certiorari was denied, 446 US 907 (1983).
53. 728 F2d 89 (2nd Cir., 1984).
54. 757 F2d 1359 (2nd Cir., 1985) at 1362.
55. 621 F Supp 842 (SDNY, 1985) at 877.
56. 347 US 227 (1954) at 229.
57. See United States v. Barshov, 733 F2d 842 (11th Cir., 1984).
58. _____P2d_____ (Alas., April 27, 1987); see NLJ (May 18, 1987) at 8.

59. See Rogers v. United States, 422 US 35 (1975), and United States v. Bear Ribs, Jr., 722 F2d 420 (8th Cir., 1983).

60. 18 USC 1501 to 1515 (1982).

61. See, for example, United States v. Presser, 187 F Supp 64 (ND Ohio, 1960).

62. See Chandler v. Florida, 449 US 560 (1981).

63. 743 F2d 1533 (11th Cir., 1984) at 1537.

64. 467 US 1025 (1984).

65. 427 US 539 (1976) at 554–555.

66. 384 US 333 (1966).

67. See Bashor v. Risly, 730 F2d 1128 (9th Cir., 1984), cert den 105 S Ct 137 (1984).

68. Infra note 56.

69. Id. at 358.

70. Id. at 358–362.

71. See Dimick v. Schiedt, 55 S Ct 296 (1935) at 297. Also note Trial Magazine (September 1987) at 76 et seq.

72. 90 S Ct 733 (1970).

73. Note the dissent of Justice Rehnquist in Park Lane Hosiery Co. Inc. v. Shore, 99 S Ct 645 (1979) at 657–658:

The founders of our Nation considered the right of trial by jury in civil cases an important bulwark against tyranny and corruption, a safeguard too precious to be left to the whim of the sovereign, or, it might be added, to that of the judiciary. Those who passionately advocated the right to a civil jury trial did not do so because they considered the jury a familiar procedural device that should be continued; the concerns for the institution of a jury trial that led to passage of the Declaration of Independence and to the Seventh Amendment were not animated by a belief that use of juries would lead to more efficient judicial administration. Trial by a jury of laymen rather than by the sovereign's judges was important to the founders because juries represent the layman's common sense, the "passional elements in our nature," and thus keep the administration of law in accord with the wishes and feelings of the community.

74. 93 S Ct 2448 (1973).

75. 63 S Ct 1077 (1902).

76. Id. at 1087–1088.

77. See generally 100 Harv L rev 1363 (1987) at 1364 et seq.

78. For example, note Thompson v. Occidental Life Ins. Co., 9 Cal. 3d 904, 909, 513 P.2d 353, 355, 109 Cal. Rptr. 473, 475 (1973); Albany Motor Inn and Restaurant, Inc., v. Watkins, 85 AD2d 797, 455 NYS.2d 616, 617 (1981). Also, see *McNeill*, 160 Cal.App. 3d at 555, 206 Cal. Rptr. at 644; Quazzo, 136 Vt. 107, 109, 386 A.2d 638, 640 (1978), and In re Fanelli's Estate, 336 So.2d 631, 632–33 (Fla. Dist. Ct. App. 1976), Kaplan v. 2108–2116 Walton Ave. Realty Corp., 103 Misc. 2d 223, 226, 425 NYS.2d 765,

767 (App. Term. 1980); Quazzo, 136 Vt. at 109, 386 A.2d at 640, and Justus v. Clelland, 133 Ariz. 381, 382, 651 P.2d 1206, 1207 (Ct. App. 1982); Jacobs v. Tenneco W., Inc., 186 Cal. App. 3d 1413, 231 Cal. Rptr. 351, 352 (1986).

79. Infra note 77 at 1371 et seq.

80. See 44 U Chi L Rev 509 (1977), and 16 Va L Rev 261 (1930).

81. In Miller v. California, 413 US 15 (1973) the Court held that a necessary element for a finding of obscenity is that "the average person, applying contemporary community standards" would characterize the material as appealing to the "prurient interest."

7

The Right to Counsel and the Conduct of Attorneys and of Government

7.1 THE RIGHT TO COUNSEL GENERALLY

The Sixth Amendment provides, inter alia, that "in all criminal prosecutions, the accused shall . . . have the Assistance of Counsel for his defense."[1] According to some legal scholars, the Sixth Amendment was intended to guarantee a criminal defendant in the federal courts only the right to employ or hire counsel.[2] But the U.S. Supreme Court has interpreted the Sixth Amendment as requiring or mandating the appointment of counsel in criminal prosecutions. Beginning with its 1932 decision in Powell v. Alabama[3] and continuing through its 1938 decision in Johnson v. Zerbst[4] the highest court has recognized the right to counsel as of such a fundamental character that its denial violates not only the Sixth Amendment, but also the due process clause of the Fourteenth Amendment.[5] In 1963 the Court in Gideon v. Wainright[6] found that the Sixth Amendment guarantee of right to counsel was obligatory on the states by the Fourteenth Amendment. Here Justice Black opined: "Reason and reflection require us to recognize that in our adversary system of criminal justice, any person haled into court who is too poor to hire a lawyer cannot be assured a fair trial unless counsel is provided for him. This seems to us to be an obvious truth."[7] The concurring opinion of Justice Harlan seemed to imply that all criminal cases were not encompassed by the court's ruling; but Justice Douglas in his concurring opinion wrote:

My Brother Harlan is of the view that a guarantee of the Bill of Rights that is made applicable to the States by reason of the Fourteenth Amendment is a lesser version of that same guarantee as applied to the Federal Government. . . . But that view has not prevailed, and rights protected against state invasion by the Due Process Clause of the Fourteenth Amendment are not watered-down versions of what the Bill of Rights guarantees . . . the Constitution makes no distinction between capital and noncapital cases.[8]

Nine years later in Argersinger v. Hamlin[9] the Court struck down a Florida rule requiring that counsel be appointed only "for non-petty offenses punishable by more than six months' imprisonment"; the Court held that "absent a knowing and intelligent waiver, no person may be imprisoned for any offense, whether classified as petty, misdemeanor, or felony, unless he was represented by counsel." The highest court continued:

While there is historical support for limiting the right to trial by jury (also guaranteed by the Sixth Amendment and the Fourteenth Amendment) to "serious criminal cases," there is no such support for a similar limitation on the right to assistance of counsel. There is nothing in the language of the Sixth Amendment, its history, or in the decisions of this Court, to indicate that it was intended to embody a retraction of the right in petty offenses wherein the common law previously did require that counsel be provided. . . . The requirement of counsel may well be necessary for a fair trial even in a petty offense prosecution.[10]

In the state of New York this right of counsel is "so valued . . . [that] it has developed independent of its federal counterpart. . . . Thus, we have extended the protections afforded by our State constitution beyond those of the federal—well before certain federal rights were recognized.[11] The New York Court of Appeals in People v. Barolomeo[12] and other cases, interpreted the right to counsel to be so broad that once an attorney enters a case on behalf of a defendant in custody, or in instances where that defendant is represented by counsel on an unrelated case, the defendant may not be questioned in the absence of counsel, either with regard to that case or unrelated charges, and furthermore the defendant may not waive his right to counsel unless he affirmatively does so in the presence of counsel. The waiver must be competent, intelligent, and voluntary.[13] However, it should be observed that the criminal defendant has no Sixth Amendment right to counsel of his choice, for the State's interest outweighs generally any hardship to the defendant.[14] But, the right to counsel has been expanded in New York in instances where an interrogating officer has actual knowledge of the accused's recent unrelated arrest; actual knowledge of a recent arrest as held in People v. Bartolomeo[15] to impose on the police in New York an affirmative duty to inquire whether the accused was represented by counsel in that unrelated charge.[16]

The Minnesota Supreme Court in State v. Rubin[17] ruled that a criminal trial court cannot accept a guilty plea from an unrepresented defendant who has not even consulted with counsel about waiving his right to counsel and about pleading guilty. But, as was explained by the same court in State v. Goff[18] the state is permitted to use any prior conviction for the purpose of sentencing if the state has not been notified by the defendant as to which prior convictions were obtained in violation of her right to counsel.

It should be observed that the right to counsel has two sides, to wit: (a) the right to counsel of one's choice, provided he or she is effective and competent to practice in the jurisdiction,[19] and (b) the right to court-appointed counsel where an accused is unable to retain counsel.[20]

7.2 EFFECTIVE ASSISTANCE OF COUNSEL

The right to counsel of one's choice, provided that he or she is effective, is but one aspect of the criminal defendant's right to a speedy and fair trial guaranteed under the Sixth Amendment. But in Gideon v. Wainright[21] the highest court held that the right to counsel means that the criminal defendant is entitled to "effective" legal counsel. As early as the landmark case of Powell v. Alabama[22] the Court pointed out that the right to counsel obligation "is not discharged by an assignment at such time or under such circumstances as to preclude the giving of effective aid in the preparation and trial of the case." And yet "those most responsible for implementing the right to counsel— trial judges, appellate courts, the law schools, the bar—are still 'papering over' the problem of inadequate assistance.[23] There is understandably some reluctance to censure the trial court, to force the trial judge to intervene whenever possible error is being committed, to lead appellate courts to "second-guess" defense tactics with the benefit of hindsight, to make lawyers more reluctant to accept court assignments, or to encourage lawyers with desperate cases to deliberately commit errors.[24] The so-called "mockery of justice" test, employed by many courts, is that representation by counsel is deemed "ineffective" only when the defense is so poor as to reduce the trial to a farce or render the trial a mockery of justice.[25] It would appear that the test of "effective assistance of counsel" should be "whether counsel exhibited the normal and customary degree of skill possessed by attorneys fairly learned and skilled in criminal law who have a fair amount of experience at the criminal bar. In applying the standard to particular actions or omissions of counsel, the relevant question should be whether counsel's behavior was such that reasonably competent and fairly experienced criminal defense lawyers might find room for debate about its propriety. If so, ineffective assistance should not be found."[26] In Beasley v. United States[27] the Fourth U.S. Court of Appeals required counsel to be "reasonably likely to render and rendering reasonably effective assistance." And in Burger v. Kemp[28] the U.S. Supreme Court ruled that a convicted murderer was not denied a fair trial because his lawyer's partner represented a co-defendant; the assistance of counsel was deemed to be "effective" assistance of counsel. It has been contended that effective assistance of counsel is undermined by the government's refusal under an informant's privilege to disclose inculpatory evidence.[29]

But in the 1988 New York case of People v. Fogarty[30] the defendant's conviction was vacated because the trial court found that (a) defendant's attorney had failed to make discovery requests; (b) had refused to participate in the voir dire of the jury; (c) had asked prosecution witnesses absurd questions; and (d) had elicited damaging testimony from his own witnesses. Under these circumstances counsel's representation violated the defendant's rights under both the New York "meaningful representation" standard and the U.S. Supreme Court's holding in Strickland v. Washington[31] to the effect that a conviction may be vacated when counsel's representation falls below an "objective standard of reasonableness," i.e., there is a "reasonable probability that, but for counsel's unprofessional errors, the result of the proceedings would have been different." According to the New York court,

Applying the standards of either the courts of the State of New York or the Supreme Court of the United States, it is clear that defense counsel, a mature and sincere person who may have had many decades of experience as a civil practitioner, had little or no familiarity with criminal law or procedure and was totally ineffective in the handling of the criminal case (see People v. Droz, 39 NY2d 457 [1976]; People v. Wagner, 104 AD2d 457 [2nd Dept., 1984]; People v. Moore, 102 AD2d 898 [2nd Dept., 1984]). It is apparent that the defense attorney had no real strategy and that his mishandling of his client's defense went beyond "mere losing tactics" (People v. Baldi supra at 146.) [A]t the very least, the right of a defendant to be represented by an attorney means more than just having a person with a law degree nominally represent him upon a trial and ask questions. Moreover, and this is well settled, the defendant's right to representation does entitle him to have counsel "conduct appropriate investigations, both factual and legal, to determine if matters of defense can be developed, and to allow himself time for reflection and preparation for trial."

Another important aspect of "effective assistance of counsel," bordering also on the issue of "choice of counsel," is seen in United States v. Monsanto[32] where the Second U.S. Court of Appeals ruled that the government may prevent defendants from hiring the lawyers of their choice by freezing defendants' assets in racketeering and drug cases. Under the Comprehensive Forfeiture Act of 1984 the government obtained a court order prohibiting the defendant from disposing of certain property pending the outcome of the criminal trial. Defendant argued that he needed the property to pay for his lawyer, and that the government's action violated his Sixth Amendment right to the counsel of his choice and his right to effective assistance of counsel. But the court took the position that even legitimate fees of defense lawyers were not exempt from the Act, provided that in an adversarial hearing the government could prove the "likelihood" that the defendant would be found guilty and that the seized assets of the defendant were the very products of the crime charged: "It would be unfair if a defendant could retain private counsel solely because he possesses tainted funds as a result of criminal activity. . . . Clearly, he would thus attain a benefit not available to indigent defendants who do not have tainted funds at their disposal." The lone dissenting opinion stressed the importance of

permitting defense counsel to perform their proper role in our adversary system of justice. . . . By failing to credit the institutional interests in a fair adversarial system, the majority opinion provides the Government with a negative, indeed an unwholesome, power over the defendant's choice of counsel in the very type of complex criminal case where astute, experienced counsel is most needed. . . . Surely this statute (Comprehensive Forfeiture Act of 1984) not only intrudes upon the individual's right to secure counsel of his choice, but it shakes the very foundation of our criminal justice system.

The contrary view is seen in the Fourth U.S. Court of Appeals 1987 decision in United States v. Harvey[33] which held that the ability to choose counsel was so important that bona fide attorney fees could be paid from potentially forfeitable tainted funds. The Fifth U.S. Court of Appeals in United States v. Thier[34] had in 1986 taken a similar view that restraining orders must be based upon such standards as irreparable harm and a balancing of the respective interests of the government and the defendant.[35] In January 1988 the Fourth U.S. Court of Appeals in United States v. Caplan & Drysdale[36] reversed its earlier ruling in United States v. Harvey[37] and held that not only is a criminal defendant prohibited from using assets allegedly derived from criminal activity to pay attorney's fees, but also that any ill-gotten assets paid to an attorney during the course of his or her representation may be seized pursuant to a post-indictment restraining order. It is submitted that this restraint is much greater than that imposed by the Second U.S. Court of Appeals in the Monsanto case.[38]

Effective assistance of counsel was a prime argument in seeking to reverse the conviction of defendant in People v. Brown;[39] defendant had been convicted of murder and robbery arising from a 1981 attack on a Brink's armored truck. Initially, defendant was represented by an attorney who allegedly was at one time associated with the Weather Underground (together with defendant), but that attorney withdrew claiming that she could not represent defendant because defendant had furnished information to law enforcement officials. A second attorney was appointed to represent defendant, and defendant appealed his conviction on the ground that there were conflicts of interest between himself and his first attorney. But the New York Appellate Division, 2nd Dept, stated:

It has been held that the right to the effective assistance of counsel may be impaired where the defense counsel represents interests which may be in conflict with those of the defendant. The defendant alleges that the attorneys that represented him prior to Mr. Isseks were more concerned with the interests of the "Movement" than with the interests of the defendant. . . . Though Ms. Williams's request for permission to withdraw as counsel upon learning that the defendant provided information to Federal agents may be an indication that she was interested in the success of the "Movement," there has been on showing that this interest created a conflict which bore a relaionship to the defense. . . . Thus the defendant's constitutional right to the effective assistance of counsel was not violated.

7.3 COURT-APPOINTED COUNSEL

What happens if the accused in a criminal proceeding is unable to secure counsel on his own, whether or not he or she has the monies to pay for the assistance of counsel? The U.S. Supreme Court case of Johnson v. Zerbst[40] proclaimed that the Sixth Amendment imposed a duty on the federal courts to appoint counsel for a defendant who is unable to retain counsel of his own. But an indigent defendant who obtains a court-appointed counsel is nevertheless obligated to repay the government, state or federal, for defense costs, as illustrated in Fuller v. Oregon.[41] Here the highest court upheld an Oregon recoupment statute authorizing reimbursement to the state for the cost of appointed defense counsel to be made a condition of probation when, after conviction, an indigent defendant is financially able to do so.[42] The Court rejected an equal protection of the law challenge, based upon the fact that the Oregon statute applied only to convicted defendants: "Oregon could surely decide with objective rationality that when a defendant has been forced to submit to a criminal prosecution that does not end in conviction, he will be freed of any potential liability to reimburse the State for the costs of his defense."

It should be noted that there is no right to court-appointed counsel in federal petty offense proceedings if the defendant is not actually incarcerated.[43] But in United States v. Leavitt[44] the Ninth U.S. Court of Appeals, relying upon Rule 44(a) of the Federal Rules of Criminal Procedure, found that a defendant convicted of careless driving in a national park, an offense carrying a maximum punishment of a $500 fine and/or six months in jail, was still entitled to a court-appointed counsel; he was given a ninety-day suspended sentence and placed on three-years probation. To the same effect is United States v. Ramirez,[45] where a defendant convicted of marijuana possession on federal land, an offense punishable by a $500 fine and/or six months in jail, was entitled to court-appointed counsel, even though he was actually placed on six-months probation and fined but $50.

The Kansas Supreme Court in Stephen v. Smith[46] ruled that the system of appointing lawyers to represent indigent defendants was a violation of the equal protection clauses of both the U.S. Constitution and the Kansas Constitution:

> The State of Kansas has the obligation to furnish counsel for indigents charged with felonies, for indigents charged with misdemeanors when imprisonment upon conviction is a real possibility, and for other persons upon certain circumstances. The state also has an obligation to pay appointed counsel such sums as will fairly compensate the attorney, not at the top rate an attorney might charge, but at a rate which is not confiscatory considering overhead and expenses.
>
> The basis of the amount to be paid for services must not vary with each judge, but there must be a statewide basis or scale. No one attorney must be saddled with appointments which unreasonably interfere with the attorney's right to make a living. Out-of-pocket expenses must be fully reimbursed.

The Nevada Supreme Court in Waters v. Barr[47] opined in an unrelated matter concerning membership in the State bar for a prosecution attorney, which activity somewhat follows in the same tradition as defense counsel:

> The regulation of the legal profession is a proper exercise of state power, and that power includes the authority to impose sanctions for any misconduct of federal prosecutors practicing law within the state, at least if the misconduct impacts improperly and adversely upon our courts or upon the practicing bar of the state.

7.4 WAIVER OF THE RIGHT TO COUNSEL

In 1966 in the landmark case of Miranda v. Arizona[48] the U.S. Supreme Court held that a confession elicited without informing a suspect of his Fifth Amendment rights against self-incrimination was not admissible as evidence in criminal proceedings against him. Implicit therein is also the right to counsel under the Sixth Amendment, although in Moran v. Burbine[49] the highest court, just twenty years later, seemed to have ruled that the defendant had waived that constitutional right to counsel. Here a suspect's pre-arraignment confession was elicited subsequent to an "otherwise valid waiver" of the suspect's rights, and the confession was held to be admissible in evidence against the suspect.[50] Justice O'Connor, writing for the six-member majority of the court, concluded that police treatment of an attorney is irrelevant to the compulsion experienced by the defendant, and furthermore does not implicate Miranda's values. The dissent of Justice Stevens, citing Escobedo v. Illinois[51] argued that "the police also prevented the attorney from consulting with his client. Independent of any other constitutional proscription, this action constitutes a violation of the Sixth Amendment right to the assistance of counsel, and excludes any statement obtained in its wake." The dissent's view was simply that no waiver of the right to counsel had taken place; but the majority opinion written by Justice O'Connor pointed out that the Sixth Amendment right to counsel attaches only after the initiation of formal adversary proceedings.[52] Indeed, according to the majority of the Court, the purpose of the Sixth Amendment is not to protect the attorney-client relationship but to ensure representation for a criminal suspect against the "prosecutorial forces of organized society," and that this right attaches only after the adversary proceedings have commenced. It was incorrect "to say that the Sixth Amendment right to counsel attaches at different times depending on the fortuity of whether the suspect or his family happens to have retained counsel prior to interrogation."[53] The dissent of Justice Stevens, however, stressed the difference between the abstract offer to call an unknown attorney (which is broadly given to all suspects under the Miranda case) and the offer never given the criminal defendant to speak with an immediately available and identifiable attorney. The dissent concluded that the government had not met its heavy burden of proving the validity of the defendant's alleged waiver of his right to counsel. Communications with counsel by a criminal defendant are so important to effective representation at trial; the role of the lawyer is that of safeguarding the rights of the criminal defendant and must also be protected. The court, by emphasizing the state's substantial interest in incommunicado custodial interrogation and failing to condemn official deception here, had denied the criminal defendant his right to counsel under the Sixth Amendment.

7.5 CONDUCT OF LAWYERS

Criminal defense counsel whose "assistance" to the criminal defendant left much to be desired have argued that any legal malpractice action against them is collaterally estopped[54] or otherwise barred because the criminal defendant failed to raise on appeal the issue of their ineffectiveness or because the issue was decided adversely to the criminal defendant in post-trial proceedings.[55] In Strickland v. Washington[56] the U.S. Supreme Court in 1984 applied a legal negligence standard of care to such an instance of "ineffective assistance of counsel," and accepted a collateral estoppel defense. And in McCord v. Bailey[57] the federal appellate court dismissed a legal negligence action by the convicted Watergate burglar: "The circumstances of this case particularly favor invocation of collateral estoppel. McCord had every incentive in his criminal proceedings to argue aggressively for his claim of ineffective assistance of counsel. . . . He had a full and fair opportunity to prove his case. . . . Estoppel saves the defendant's lawyers from the burden of defending a lawsuit on an issue that has already been fully adjudicated."[58]

In Spring v. Constantino[59] the Connecticut Supreme Court refused accord immunity from suit for public defenders or any other attorney representing a criminal defendant: "The function . . . does not afford a basis upon which the cloak of judicial immunity may be extended. Nor does the policy behind the doctrine of judicial immunity require that it be applied to a public defender who is like any other attorney whose duties as an officer of the court and to an individual client and 'whose principled and fearless' conduct of the defense are not deterred by the prospect of liability."[60]

A disciplinary rule of the Virginia Supreme Court restricted lawyer's comments about pending litigation, but the Fourth U.S. Court of Appeals in Hirschkop v. Snead[61] found no constitutional objection to the rule; it did not violate First Amendment rights of attorneys insofar as it applied to criminal jury trials, and the rule was not constitutionally infirm because of its failure to limit the ban on lawyer's comments to those instances where the comments posed a serious and imminent threat to the criminal defendant's right to a fair trial. But in Chicago Council of Lawyers v. Bauer[62] another federal appellate court ruled that a portion of the local criminal rule of the district court proscribing lawyers' extrajudicial comments during selection of jury at trial relating to the trial, the parties, or the issues in trial can be the basis for a presumption of a serious and imminent threat to the fair administration of justice. The constitutional infirmity arose from the fact that they restricted communications other than those which posed a serious and imminent threat to the administration of justice.

7.6 CONDUCT OF GOVERNMENT

The Sixth Amendment guarantee of the right to counsel is frequently implicated in instances where the government employs informants to ferret out incriminating statements from criminal suspects in the absence of counsel.[63] In Massiah v. United States[64] the government had surreptitiously interrogated an indicted defendant through the use of a co-defendant who was cooperating with the government. The incriminating statements made to the co-defendant were overheard by a government agent through a radio transmitter that had been installed in the automobile of the cooperating co-defendant. The U.S. Supreme Court found that the criminal defendant's right to counsel was violated for he "was denied the basic protections of that guarantee (i.e., the right to counsel) when there was used against him at his trial evidence of his own incriminating words, which federal agents had deliberately elicited from him after he had been indicted and in the absence of counsel."[65] The Court stressed that the Sixth Amendment related equally to indirect and surreptitious interrogation as well as to direct questioning in the jail. In Brewer v. Williams,[66] involving the murder of a ten-year-old girl by a former mental patient, the criminal defendant was interrogated on the train as to the location of the girl's body, and the criminal defendant responded accordingly. His counsel had requested that the criminal defendant not be questioned until he had conferred with counsel. The court found violation of right to counsel in that the adversary proceedings had begun, and therefore the elicited testimony was inadmissible in evidence. Indeed, the defendant's right to counsel had attached just prior to the time that the detective on the train had made an appeal to the criminal defendant's "religion" the reason for his incriminating statement.

In United States v. Henry[67] in 1980 the criminal defendant admitted his participation in a robbery to his cellmate who had served as a government informant and who later testified at the trial against the defendant. The court reversed the conviction on the ground that his right to counsel had been violated by the government's conduct which may not have been "deliberate" but had the same effect.

NOTES

1. See generally 20 U of San Fran L Rev (Winter 1986) at 317 et seq.
2. See 93 Harv L Rev 1 (1979) at 83.

3. 287 US 45 (1932)
4. 304 US 458 (1938).
5. See Chapter 3 herein.
6. 372 US 335 (1963).
7. The Court continued:

Governments, both state and federal, quite properly spend vast sums of money to establish machinery to try defendants accused of crime. Lawyers to prosecute are everywhere
deemed essential to protect the public's interest in an orderly society. Similarly, there
are few defendants charged with crime, few indeed, who fail to hire the best lawyers
they can get to prepare and present their defenses. That government hires lawyers to
prosecute and defendants who have the money hire lawyers to defend are the strongest
indications of the widespread belief that lawyers in criminal courts are necessities, not
luxuries. . . . From the very beginning, our state and national constitutions and laws
have laid great emphasis on procedural and substantive safeguards designed to assure
fair trials before impartial tribunals in which every defendant stands equal before the
law. This noble ideal cannot be realized if the poor man charged with crime has to face
his accusers without a lawyer to assist him.

8. Id.
9. 407 US 25 (1972).
10. Justice Douglas concluded:

We are by no means convinced that legal and constitutional questions involved in a case
that actually leads to imprisonment even for a brief period are any less complex than
when a person can be sent off for six months or more. [Moreover], the volume of
misdemeanor cases, far greater in number than felony prosecutions, may create an ob-
session for speedy dispositions, regardless of the fairness of the result. . . .
    We must conclude, therefore, that the problems associated with misdemeanor and
petty offenses often require the presence of counsel to insure the accused a fair trial. [In
his concurring opinion], Mr. Justice Powell suggests that these problems are raised even
in situations where there is no prospect of imprisonment. We need not consider the
requirements of the Sixth Amendment as regards the right to counsel where loss of
liberty is not involved, however, for here, petitioner was in fact sentenced to jail. . . .
    Under the rule we announce today, every judge will know when the trial of a mis-
demeanor starts that no imprisonment may be imposed, even though local law permits
it, unless the accused is represented by counsel. He will have a measure of the seriousness and gravity of the offense and therefore know when to name a lawyer to represent
the accused before the trial starts.

11. Note People v. Settles, 46 NY2d 154 (1987).
12. 53 NY2d 225 (1981).
13. People v. Hobson, infra note 10.2.
14. People v. Jackson, _____NYS2d_____ (Nassau County, March 22,
1988):

It is the determination of this court that no hearing is necessary as to the issue of representation by counsel of choice of the defendants. This decision has been made after a review of all the motion papers originally submitted to Supreme Court Justice Burke and following conferences with all parties. Dillon v. Schiavo, 114 A.D. 2d 924, app. dismissed 67 N.Y. 2d 605. The court acknowledges the undisputed fact that independent of the attached assets, defendants cannot afford the payment of legal fees to their retained attorneys in the instant case. Moreover, the court adopts the findings of the Supreme Court in its entirety in that the claiming authority has established a substantial probability of success on the merits and that the assets of the defendants are readily removable from the jurisdiction. Based upon the establishment of these two factors, it is clear that the interest of the State in attaching the defendants assets far outweigh any hardship the defendants may claim by not retaining the specific counsel of their choice.

Defendants have argued that by attaching the assets of the defendants, the district attorney has rendered the defendants indigent, thus denying them their right to counsel of their choice under the Sixth Amendment of the United States. Such an assertion is incorrect as a matter of law.

Neither the United States Constitution, nor the New York Constitution establishes a constitutional right to retain a particular attorney of the defendant's chosing. In the recent case of Kuriansky v. Bed. Stuy. Health Care Corporation, et al. _____A.D. 2d _____ (February 16, 1988) the Second Department addressed this issue in relation to the use of provisional remedies as permitted under Article 13A of the CPLR. . . .

Although New York State is presently without case law as to the right to counsel of choice under Article 13A of the CPLR, several federal courts have analyzed the Federal Comprehensive Forfeiture Act (21 U.S. C. sec 853 (e)(1)(A) [sic] in relation to this issue. In United States v. Caplin and Drysdale, _____F.2d_____no 86-5050 4th Cir. Jan 11, 1988 (en banc) the Fourth Circuit Court of Appeals held that "the right to counsel of choice belongs only to those with legitimate assets. The right to counsel does not guarantee that every defendant will have the lawyer he desires."

In United States v. Mosanto, _____F.2d_____ (2nd Cir., Dec. 21, 1987) the Second Circuit Court of Appeals directed the District Court to hold a hearing before a forefeiture of the assets required to retain counsel. The Second Circuit further held that the government bears the burden of the possibility that it will prevail at the trial as to the criminal liability of the defendants.

However, in the case at bar there is no need for a hearing of this nature. Under [sic] the provisional remedies permitted in Article 13A of the CPLR, Justice Burke has already determined there is a substantial likelihood of success on the merits and that there is a high probability of conviction of the defendants.

15. Infra note 10.2.

16. Note also People v. Woolard, 137 NY MIsc2d 763 (1987), People v. Lucarano, 61 NY2d 138 (1984), and People v. Claudio, 59 NY2d 556 (1983).

17. _____NW 2d_____ (Jan 22, 1988).

18. _____NW 2d_____ (Minn, July 31, 1987).

19. See Section 7.2 herein.

20. See Section 7.3 herein.

21. Infra note 6.

22. Infra note 3.

23. See Bazelon, "The Defective Assistance of Counsel," 42 U Cinn L Rev 1 (1973).

24. See 59 Northwest U L Rev 289 (1964).

25. Infra note 16 at 28.

26. See Finer, "Ineffective Assistance of Counsel," 58 Cornell L Rev 1077 (1973) at 1080.

27. 491 F2d 687 (6th Cir., 1974).

28. 55 USLW 5131 (1987).

29. See Roviaro v United States, 353 US 53 (1956), and McCray v. Illinois, 386 US 300 (1966).

30. _____NYS 2d_____ (New York County, January 12, 1988).

31. 466 US 668 (1984).

32. _____F2d_____ (2nd Cir., January 3, 1988).

33. 814 F2d 905 (4th Cir., 1987).

34. 801 F2d 1463 (5th Cir., 1986).

35. See NLJ (January 18, 1988) at 3.

36. _____F2d_____ (4th Cir., January 1988).

37. Infra note 26.

38. Infra note 25.

39. _____AD2d_____, _____NYS2d_____ (March 7, 1988).

40. Infra note 4.

41. 417 US 40 (1974).

42. The highest court stressed that:

the recoupment statute is quite clearly directed only at those convicted defendants who are indigent at the time of the criminal proceedings against them but who subsequently gain the ability to pay the expenses of legal representation. Defendants with no likelihood of having the means to repay are not put under even a conditional obligation to do so, and those upon whom a conditional obligation is imposed are not subjected to collection procedures until their indigency has ended and no "manifest hardship" will result.

43. See United States v. Jackson, 605 F2d 1319 (4th Cir., 1979).

44. 608 F2d 1290 (9th Cir., 1979); also see note 1 at 328.

45. 555 F Supp 736 (ED Cal., 1983).

46. 747 P2d 816 (Kan, 1987).

47. 747 Pd 900 (Nev, 1987).

48. 384 US 436 (1966).

49. 106 S Ct 1135 (1986); also see Harv L Rev 100 (1986) at 125.

50. Id. at 126:

On June 29, 1977, police officers from Cranston, Rhode Island, arrested Brian Burbine and his two companions for breaking and entering. Based upon information from an informant and from Burbine's companions, the Cranston police came to suspect Burbine in the unsolved Providence murder of a woman named Mary Jo Hickey. While Burbine was detained that evening, his sister telephoned the public defender's office to obtain legal counsel for her brother. As a result, an assistant public defender telephoned the police station, identified herself, and stated that she would act as Burbine's legal counsel. The police told her that Burbine would not be questioned that evening. She was not informed that Burbine had become a suspect in the Providence murder investigation or that the Providence police were at the Cranston station. Burbine was never informed of his attorney's efforts to contact him. Within an hour, the police began a series of interrogations of the suspect. After being informed of his *Miranda* rights, Burbine eventually executed three written waivers and confessed to the murder. At no point during the interrogation did he request an attorney.

Prior to trial, Burbine moved to suppress the confessions. The trial court denied the motion, and the jury found Burbine guilty of murder. He appealed to the Supreme Court of Rhode Island, which affirmed the lower court's decision by a 3–2 vote. Burbine unsuccessfully petitioned the United States District Court for the District of Rhode Island for a writ of habeas corpus and then appealed to the Court of Appeals for the First Circuit, alleging that the confessions were elicited in violation of his rights under the fifth, sixth, and fourteenth amendments. The court of appeals reversed, holding that the police's failure to inform Burbine's attorney of their plans to interrogate him and their failure to inform Burbine of the attorney's telephone call violated his fifth amendment right to counsel and privilege against self-incrimination.

51. 378 US 478 (1964).

52. 106 S Ct at 1145-1146 (1986).

53. Id.

54. See Warren Freedman, Res Judicata and Collateral Estoppel (Quorum Books, 1987).

55. See Trial Magazine (September 1987) at 35 et seq.

56. 104 S Ct 2052 (1984).

57. 636 F2d 606 (DC Cir., 1981), cert den 101 S Ct 2314 (1981).

58. Id. at 610.

59. 362 A2d 871 (Conn., 1975).

60. Id.

61. 594 F2d 356 (4th Cir., 1979).

62. 522 F2d 242 (7th Cir., 1975).

63. See generally Garcia, "The Right to Counsel and Informants." Case & Comment (May–June 1987) at 21 et seq.

64. 377 US 201 (1964).

65. Id. at 206.

66. 430 US 387 (1977).

67. 447 US 264 (1980).

8

Grand Jury
Investigations and
Other Pre-Trial
Proceedings

8.1 INTRODUCTION

The constitutional right to a fair and a speedy criminal trial is often questioned in grand jury investigations and other pre-trial proceedings. In People v. Washington Guevara[1] the prosecutor, during the second half of the pre-trial suppression hearing, moved to have two unidentified men and a woman excluded from the courtroom "based upon his assertion that the complainant and several witnesses had been threatened because of their participation in the criminal proceedings involving the defendant." Defense counsel objected, arguing that spectators should not be excluded merely because of their "appearance." The trial court "directed the men to leave without any further inquiry." The defendant was convicted of attempted murder in the second degree, assault in the first degree, criminal possession of a weapon in the second degree, and criminal possession of a weapon in the third degree. The New York Appellate Division, 2nd Dept., in 1987 ordered a new public suppression hearing and observed:

The right to a public trial applies to pre-trial proceedings. . . . Although the defendant's right to a public trial may be overcome upon a showing of an overriding interest that is likely to be prejudiced if the courtroom remains open, the representations proffered by the prosecutor here were insufficient to justify closure of the courtroom for the remainder of the pre-trial hear-

ing. . . . Moreover, the exclusion of the two unidentified men was not pre-
ceded by "an inquiry careful enough to assure the court that the defendant's
right to a public trial is not being sacrificed for less than compelling reasons. . . . The mere fact that one other person remained in the courtroom
during the hearing and that the subsequent trial was completely public, is
immaterial. . . . The fact that the court could have reasonably concluded that
no prejudice would result to the defendant as a result of the closing is wholly
irrelevant. It is well established that a defendant is not required to prove specific prejudice in order to obtain relief for a violation of the public trial guarantee since the closing of the courthouse doors results in an intangible loss to
society at large.[2]

It might also be observed that the constitutional right to a speedy
trial might not be in the best interest of the criminal defendant.[3] A
truly speedy trial, from a pragmatic viewpoint, may conflict with defense attorney's scheduling concerns and accord him/her insufficient
time to prepare a client's case for trial. On the other hand, the prosecutor may not want to move too rapidly either, witness the prosecutor's new device known as the "superseding indictment,"[4] which delays the trial and allows the government post-indictment recourse to
the grand jury to prepare the case for trial. The prosecutor can by this
device of the "superseding indictment" cure defects in its case and
even change the entire indictment. However, in United States v.
Freeman[5] the federal district court for the Southern District of New
York supported defense counsels' vigorous demand for a speedy trial
when the court unmasked the "superseding indictment" as a "tactic"
to give the prosecutor more time to the detriment of the defendant's
constitutional right to a speedy trial. Under the Speedy Trial Act of
1974[6] the indictment must be issued within thirty days of arrest; but,
under Section 3288 of Title 18 of U.S. Code, if an indictment is returned before the expiration of the statute of limitations and is later
dismissed for any "error, defect, or irregularity with respect to the
grand jury," the government is given additional time to comply with
the statute of limitations.[7] And the government may present a "superseding indictment" to a new grand jury without that new grand jury
hearing a single witness or seeing any exhibits.[8] The Speedy Trial Act
of 1974 expressly excludes the time necessary for the government to
file the "superseding indictment."[9] It should be clear that there is
fundamental unfairness to a criminal defendant in being required to
disclose the "defect" in the initial indictment only to have it cured by

a "superseding indictment."[10] Justice for the criminal defendant, however, can be done, as illustrated in U.S. v. Fields,[11] where the defendant was charged with distributing controlled substances. The government moved orally to dismiss the indictment on the ground that it could not vouch for the credibility of an essential witness. Defendant opposed a dismissal without prejudice, but the initial court nevertheless dismissed the indictment without prejudice. When the defendant was re-indicted, the later court realized that the government had never intended to use the "essential witness," and that without his testimony the government had no case against the defendant. Accordingly, the court dismissed the second indictment with prejudice.

8.2 GRAND JURY INVESTIGATIONS GENERALLY

Over fifteen years ago a Lousiville, Kentucky, news reporter wrote an article describing his observations of two local residents synthesizing hashish from marijuana. He appeared before a grand jury in response to a summons, but refused, despite the trial court's order, to identify those persons he had seen possessing marijuana or making hashish. He then wrote another newspaper article recounting interviews with and observations of unnamed drug users. He refused to respond to that inquiry after being served with a grand jury subpoena. In both instances the Kentucky Court of Appeals rejected his claim of freedom of the press under the First Amendment. The U.S. Supreme Court in Branzburg v. Hayes,[12] in an opinion by Justice Byron White, affirmed: "Here petitioner refused to answer questions that directly related to criminal conduct which he had observed and written about. . . . In both cases, what petitioner wrote was true; he had direct information to provide the grand jury concerning the commission of serious crimes."[13] The dissent of Justice Douglas was based upon his finding that there was no

"compelling need" that can be shown by the Government which qualifies the reporter's immunity from appearing or testifying before a grand jury, unless the reporter himself is implicated in a crime. His immunity . . . is therefore quite complete, for absent his involvement in a crime, the First Amendment protects him against an appearance before a grand jury, and if he is involved in a crime, the Fifth Amendment stands as a barrier. Since . . . there is no area of inquiry not protected by a privilege, the reporter need not appear for

the futile purpose of invoking one to each question. And . . . [since] newsman has an absolute right not to appear before a grand jury, it follows that
. . . a journalist who voluntarily appears before that body may invoke his
First Amendment privilege to specific questions.[14]

It should be noted that the ancient role of the grand jury involved
the dual function of determining if there is probable cause to believe
that a crime had been committed and of protecting citizens against
unfounded criminal prosecutions. Today the dual function of the grand
jury has not changed; testimonial compulsion is at the heart of the
grand jury's role in the criminal justice system. The nature of grand
jury testimony was recently explored by the Second U.S. Court of
Appeals in U.S. v. Esposito[15]. Here defendant was convicted for criminal contempt for his refusal to testify before a grand jury, and his
defense centered about "duress," i.e., he cited the testimony of an
FBI agent that two men indicted by another grand jury (in New Jersey)
had beaten him and that he feared reprisal. But the federal appellate
court affirmed his conviction for criminal contempt:

The record here indicates that Esposito had actual possession of transcripts
prior to trial. His counsel repeatedly referred to and recited from New Jersey
proceedings in seeking Esposito's release from jail following his civil contempt conviction nearly four months before the indictment in this case was
returned. . . . Even if the government suppressed documents, Esposito would
be entitled to a new trial only "if there is a reasonable probability that, had
the evidence been disclosed to the defense, the result of the proceeding would
have been different." Here, the allegedly suppressed materials do not support
a duress defense which requires "actual or threatened force of such a nature
as to induce a well-founded fear of impending death or serious bodily harm"
coupled with no reasonable opportunity to escape the compulsion without
committing a crime. . . . Thus, we hold there was no suppression . . . because at all times Esposito knew or had access to facts which he claimed the
government had suppressed.[16]

It should also be noted that the names and addresses of jurors are
confidential and exempt from public disclosure requirements of a state's
Freedom of Information Law as in the State of New York, In Matter
of Newsday.[17] The New York Court of Appeals here unanimously
affirmed a lower court decision in which a newspaper was denied access to that information in a murder trial. Jury records fall within the

confidentiality provisions of the New York Judiciary Law which prohibits the disclosure of juror qualifications questionnaires unless an application for release of special information in the questionnaires is properly submitted to the Appellate Division: "It is the information from the questionnaires, not the forms themselves which, if made public, could invade jurors' privacy interests and threaten their safety."

The sanctity of the grand jury proceedings is seen in United States v. Haller[18] where the Second U.S. Court of Appeals took the necessary steps "to protect the secrecy of sensitive matters affecting a grand jury proceeding and an ongoing criminal investigation." The federal appellate court continued:

The Supreme Court has "recognized that the proper functioning of our grand jury system depends upon the secrecy of grand jury proceedings." *Douglas Oil Co. v. Petrol Stops Northwest*, 441 U.S. 211, 218 (1979). Among other things, if matters relating to grand jury proceedings became public, prospective witnesses may be deterred from testifying, those who do testify may be less likely to do so truthfully, targets of investigations may flee, and persons who are the subject of an ultimately meritless investigation may face public embarrassment. See *id.* at 219 and n.10; *United States v. Procter & Gamble Co.*, 356 U.S. 677, 681–82 n.6 (1958). To guard against such consequences, Fed. R. Crim. P.6(e)(2) provides for the nondisclosure of matters occuring before a grand jury. Moreover, Fed. R. Crim. P.6 (e)(5), which provides for the closure of hearings on "matters affecting a grand jury proceeding," was added in 1983 in order to "make it clear that certain hearings which would reveal matters which have previously occurred before a grand jury *or are likely to occur before a grand jury with respect to a pending or on-going investigation* must be conducted in camera in whole or in part in order to prevent public disclosure of such secret information." Fed. R. Crim. P.6(e)(5) advisory committee's note (emphasis added) . . . not specifically named were reasonably identifiable from paragraph four, to public embarrassment, even if they were later exonerated by the grand jury. *Cf. In re New York Times*, 828 F. 2d at 115 (trial judge should consider privacy interests of innocent third parties before unsealing Title III material); *opinion after remand, In re New York Times*, Nos. 87–1422, 87–1450 (2d Cir. Dec. 10, 1987) (per curiam). Protection of such privacy interests is especially important when the third parties under investigation may be unaware of the threatened danger to their interests and may not appear before the district court to protect themselves. We believe, therefore, that preservation of grand jury secrecy and the sensitivity of an ongoing criminal investigation were "higher values" justifying sealing and that redaction of paragraph four was "narrowly tailored to serve [those] interest[s]." *Press-Enterprise II*, 106 S.Ct. at 2743.

The New York Appellate Division, 2nd Dept., in People v. Banville[19] in the same tone, discussed the validity of a waiver on the part of the criminally accused of the indictment and a willingness to proceed by way of a court information. The court pointed out that the New York legislature "has spoken unequivocally that a waiver may be effected at any time prior to the filing of an indictment by the Grand Jury." In short, "once an indictment has been returned by the Grand Jury, any subsequent waiver is indeed untimely and hence wholly ineffective. Consequently, a plea of guilty to any other accusatory instrument encompassing crimes arising out of the transaction for which the defendant was originally indicted must also be deemed a nullity."

8.3 PROSECUTORIAL ABUSES AND THE FAIR AND SPEEDY CRIMINAL TRIAL

Professor James Vorenberg of Harvard Law School has effectively argued that prosecutorial discretion plays a pervasive role in the administration of justice, that prosecutors exercise essentially unchecked power in making decisions about charging and plea bargaining, and that these decisions determine in a large part who will be convicted and what punishments will be imposed.[20] Obviously, prosecutorial abuses also prejudice the criminal defendant's right to a fair and speedy trial, especially since prosecutors generally have uncontrolled discretional authority.[21]

A prosecutor typically plea bargains with those defendants who would be convicted if they went to trial. Much less common is the situation in which the prosecutor believes that the defendant has done something wrong but doubts his own ability to convict. The doubt may be derived from the availability or credibility of witnesses, from flaws in the admissibility of evidence or in the police investigation, from the attitude of the judge or jury toward that particular offense, or from the probability that the defendant's right to a speedy and a fair trial may be jeopardized. The prosecutor's abuse of his discretion may take any form, and "few subjects are less adapted to judicial review than the exercise . . . of his discretion in deciding when and whether to institute criminal proceedings, or what precise charge shall be made, or whether to dismiss a proceeding once brought.[22] However, in the landmark case of Yick Wo v. Hopkins[23] the highest court more than a hundred years ago struck down a prosecution for the invalid selection of a target, to wit: a Chinese laundryman who was not issued a license while Caucasians were issued licenses in San Francisco! But normally, unless prosecution is based on a constitutionally impermissible criterion such as race, sex, or exercise of First Amendment rights, the exercise of prosecutorial discretion has routinely been upheld by the courts.[24]

Prosecutorial abuse can be seen in the lack of fair process and equal treatment with respect to conviction and punishment, and once again there appears to be no methodology for testing the decision against standards. This risk of unequal treatment means that a prosecutor has almost unbridled power to act arbitrarily and capriciously for or against particular defendants.

A prosecutor has a duty to disclose promises of favorable treatment made to witnesses for the prosecution,[25] and a criminal defendant may not bribe or threaten a witness in order to obtain testimony favorable to his case.[26] A witness's testimony must not be influenced; a witness must testify according to his/her perception of the truth and not according to the wishes of the prosecutor or of the criminal defendant.[27] Otherwise, the defendant's right to a fair trial is violated. A prosecutor can coax cooperative and favorable testimony from a witness in many ways that a criminal defendant cannot, to wit: promise of immunity from prosecution, or that prosecution will be dropped or charges will be reduced, or monetary payments will be made.[28] In contrast, a criminal defendant may not offer a witness anything of value even if it were within his/her power; coercion of favorable testimony by the criminal defendant would invite widespread abuse, it is argued.[29] Therefore, a prosecutor's failure to disclose promises of favorable treatment made to witnesses may violate the due process clauses of the Fifth and Fourteenth Amendments by denying the criminal defendant a fair trial.[30] It is mandatory that a jury know of these promises in order to evaluate properly the witness's testimony. Bias or prejudice of a witness jeopardizes a fair trial. In United States v. Agurs[31] the U.S. Supreme Court established a framework for reviewing cases involving non-disclosure of impeaching or exculpatory evidence by prosecutors.[32] The responsibility of the appellate court in each instance is to determine whether the undisclosed evidence was "material," in which event its suppression mandates a remand for a new trial. For example, when a witness for the prosecution perjures himself or herself and the prosecutor knows or should have known of the perjury, the prosecutor must and has in fact an affirmative duty to correct the false testimony.[33] When defense counsel makes a pre-trial request for specific, non-privileged evidence in the prosecutor's possession, the prosecutor must produce that evidence. The highest court concluded: "The prosecutor will not have violated his constitutional duty of disclosure unless his omission is of sufficient significance to result in the denial of the defendant's right to a fair trial."[34] On the other hand, the New York Appellate Division, 1st Dept., in People v. Bagarozy[35] found "prosecutorial excesses" and reversed a conviction on two counts of sodomy. According to the court,

By seizing on defendant's trial strategy to acknowledge his homosexuality, the prosecutor was able to bring out his preference for youth, and, additionally, that this preference earned him a place in the police records of known pedophiles. The references to defendant's pedophilia were improper and the result of an erroneous ruling, since it would have been sufficient to meet the claim of homosexuality to demonstrate that a civilian complaint had led to an investigation which ultimately focused on defendant. . . . That error was then compounded by a series of questions. . . . which disclosed that defendant was "known to the police department morals division" and that he was a "known pedophile." With that evidence before the jury, defendant was deprived of whatever chance he had for a fair trial, and the application for a mistrial should have been granted.

Specifically, the New York court opined:

The issue at trial was whether defendant had engaged in several discrete acts of oral sodomy with underage youths, not the state of mind with which those acts were committed. Yet, by successfully arguing a variety of inapplicable and implausible theories of admissibility, the prosecutor was able to place before the jury a wealth of prejudicial information about defendant's deviate lifestyle and associations. As the prosecutor's summation graphically makes clear, the true purpose behind the introduction of this evidence was to expose defendant's sexual preferences and attitudes in order to demonstrate a propensity to commit the crimes charged. The use of this evidence for such a purpose was a clear violation of well-settled legal principles.

The court also concluded that

the prosecutor's invocation of Devine Authority, coupled as it was with an appeal to "the citizens of this county" to thwart NAMBLA's corruption of their youth, took the summation beyond the pale of routine oratorical excess. It was an incitement to convict on grounds that transcend the evidence and the law. The invocation of extra-legal norms in criminal prosecutions has been uniformly disapproved, because of the risk that these norms will usurp the primacy of reason and of law. (See, *People v. Wood*, 66 NY 2d 374, 381; *People v. Torres*, 111 AD 2d 885; *People v. McCloskey*, 92 AD 2d 672, 673; *People v. Williams*, 73 AD 2d 525; *People v. Fields*, 27 AD 2d 736.)

Balancing the gravity and pervasiveness of the cited errors against the weight of the admissible evidence, we cannot find that they were harmless. (See, *People v. Crimmins*, 36 NY 2d 230).

Of increasing concern in protecting the criminal defendant's right to a fair trial are prosecutorial abuses in opening and closing arguments. A failure to prove matters referred to in an opening statement is an example, but it is not reversible error should that evidence be excluded by the trial court.[36] Nor was a criminal defendant denied a fair trial by a prosecutor's remark that defense counsel were "trying to cloud the waters as squid and octopi are reputed to do."[37] But in United States v. Stefan[38] it was held that the prosecutor made improper prejudicial remarks during closing argument when he stated: "Is it reasonable to think that the government would fabricate a case with all the crime in this area?" The Eleventh U.S. Court of Appeals forbade this argument since it implied that the prosecutor reached the determination that the defendant was guilty before the trial, and therefore the jury should consider that fact. Similarly, in Jacobs v. State of Nevada[39] the state court disapproved of comments made by the prosecuting attorney in his final argument when he stated that he would "not tell the jurors to put themselves in the victim's position looking down the barrel of this shotgun because that would be improper." The state court ruled that "the prosecutor's resourceful disavowal . . . did not remedy the transgression," and the defendant's right to a fair trial was violated. But in Garofolo v. Coomb[40] the Second U.S. Court of Appeals, while agreeing that the prosecutor's remarks were inappropriate and improper, nevertheless ruled that the trial judge had cured the error by instructing the jury so that the net effect was that the improper remarks were not so prejudicial as to render the criminal trial fundamentally unfair. In United States v. Lopez[41] the prosecutor's closing argument made reference to a mask and wig which paraphernalia were unrelated to the crime charged; but the Ninth U.S. Court of Appeals opined that there was no error because the judge neutralized any potential prejudice by striking the prosecutor's statement and giving the cautionary instruction to the jury. Similarly, in United States v. Polizzi[42] the same court found that the prosecutor's exhortation for the jury to join in the war against crime and statements linking the defendants to organized crime were prejudicial, but the trial court's curative instructions to the jury were sufficient to render the prosecutor's statements harmless in terms of the defendant's right to a fair trial.

The U.S. Supreme Court in 1986 in Darden v. Wainright[43] stated that, where error tends to divert the jury's attention "from the ultimate question of guilt or innocence," the appellate courts should reverse a conviction. Here, in a capital murder trial the prosecutor in his closing statement said that the defendant "shouldn't be out of his cell unless he has a leash on him," and that he wished he could see the defendant sitting in the courtroom "with no face, blown away by a shotgun." The highest court condemned these remarks, yet concluded that these remarks of the prosecutor had not deprived the defendant of a fair trial.[44]

Rule 6(e) of the Federal Rules of Criminal Procedure expressly states that the government shall not disclose the details of a grand jury investigation to the public. In United States v. Midland Asphalt Corp.[45] the defendant had been indicted for antitrust law violations and filed a pre-trial motion to dismiss the indictment, alleging a violation by the prosecution of Rule 6(e). The federal district court denied the motion, and the Second U.S. Court of Appeals affirmed:

> The nondisclosure provisions Rule 6(e) protects society's interest in keeping secret the identity of grand jury witnesses and persons under investigation. Therefore . . . a violation of Rule 6(e) is not rendered harmless simply because the defendant is convicted; at least in some instances, the more egregious the violation to Rule 6(e) the more likely it becomes that the petit jury will convict. Accordingly, we do not believe that Mechanik precludes a federal court of appeals from exercising post-trial review of an order denying a motion to dismiss an indictment for violation of Rule 6(e). By the same token, we believe a Rule 6(e) challenge does not qualify for immediate review under the collateral order doctrine.[46]

It is well to note the American Bar Association Standards for Criminal Justice, The Prosecution Function, Standard 3-5.8, Argument to the Jury, which reads as follows:

(a) The prosecutor may argue all reasonable inferences from evidence in the record. It is unprofessional conduct for the prosecutor intentionally to misstate the evidence or mislead the jury as to the inferences it may draw. (b) It is unprofessional conduct for the prosecutor to express his or her personal belief or opinion as to the truth or falsity of any testimony or evidence of the guilt of the defendant. (c) The prosecutor should not use arguments calculated to inflame the passions or prejudices of the jury. (d) The prosecutor should refrain from argument which would divert the jury from its duty to decide the case on the evidence, by injecting issues broader than the guilt or innocence of the accused under the controlling law, or by making predictions of the consequences of the jury's verdict. (e) It is the responsibility of the court to ensure the final argument to the jury is kept within proper, accepted bounds.

Also, note Standard 17.17, Closing Argument, National District Attorneys Association, which reads as follows:

A. Counsel's closing argument to the jury should be characterized by fairness, accuracy, rationality, and a reliance upon the evidence. B. Because the prosecution bears the burden of proof, the prosecution should have the opportunity to open argument and to rebut the defense's closing argument with the order of the closing statements being prosecution, defense, and prosecution again. C. Counsel should have the discretion to comment upon the substantive law relevant to the case. D. The prosecution should have the discretion to comment upon the defense's failure to call witnesses under its control and favorable to its cause, excluding the defendant, when a name has been raised in opening statements or where defense has introduced the name or existence of an individual, the prosecutor should have the discretion to comment upon the defense's failure to call that witness.

On opening arguments of the prosecutor, reference should be made to ABA Standard 3-5.5, which reads as follows:

The prosecutor's opening statement should be confined to a brief statement of the issues in the case and to remarks on evidence the prosecutor intends to offer which the prosecutor believes in good faith will be available and admissible. It is unprofessional conduct to allude to any evidence unless there is a good faith and reasonable basis for believing that such evidence will be tendered and admitted in evidence.

And Standard 17.5 of NDAA, which reads as follows:

A. The prosecutor should be afforded the opportunity to give an opening statement for the purpose of explaining the issues before the court and the procedures of the particular trial.

B. The prosecutor should not allude to any evidence unless there is good faith and reasonable basis for believing that such evidence will be tendered and admitted into evidence at the trial.[47]

Indeed, it would appear that the prosecutor, with respect to both the opening and closing arguments may well be "walking a tightrope" as it should properly be since the burden of proof of guilt of the defendant rests squarely upon the shoulders of the prosecutor. But prosecutorial misconduct is not a byproduct of the judicial system; it is but one aspect of the defendant's right to a speedy and fair trial.

The constitutionality of "independent prosecutors"[48] is also an important issue that may infringe upon the criminal defendant's right to a fair trial. Section 2, Clause 2, of Article II of the U.S. Constitution expressly provides that "Congress may, by law, vest the appointment of such inferior officers, as they think proper . . . in the Courts of Law." More than one hundred years ago in Ex Parte Siebold[49] the U.S. Supreme Court found no constitutional barrier to an appointment of an executive officer with judicial duties.

8.4 ETHICS AND CONFLICTS OF INTEREST

The quality of a criminal defendant's representation may be impaired by conflicts of interest emanating from the natural tension between the interest of the criminal defendant and the public interest in a fair and efficient criminal justice system.[50] Ethics and professional responsibility enter where the prosecutor has a different priority for one criminal case over another criminal case. A government lawyer, for example, serves the interests of many different entities: his supervisor in the agency or department, the agency or department itself, the entire government of which the agency or department is but a part, and the public interest.[51] Although the central function of prosecutors is advocacy, most prosecutors have important decision-making responsibilities.[52] A prosecutor brings a criminal suit because he believes it should be brought, unlike a private attorney who brings a civil suit because the client believes it is proper to do so. A prosecutor must also make important political choices about how to distribute scarce public resources.[53] Prosecutors occasionally confront conflicts between their role as advocate and their performance of investigative functions.[54] Other problems in ethics may arise with respect to financial interests and even concurrent private employment, inter alia.[55]

NOTES

1. ____AD2d____, ____NYS2d____ (2nd Dept., December 15, 1987).

2. Id.

3. See generally, Cohen, "Superseding Indictments—New Device for Prosecutors," NYLJ (August 14, 1987) at 1 et seq.

4. See 8 Moore's Federal Practice, Section 7.05(1).

5. 87 Cr 293 (LLS) (SDNY, 1987).

6. See Section 4.5 herein.

7. Infra note 3.

8. See U.S. v. Schlesinger, 598 F2d 722 (2nd Cir., 1979), cert den 444 US 880 (1979).

9. Title 18, United States Code, Section 3161(h)(7).("A reasonable period of delay when the defendant is joined for trial with a co-defendant as to whom the time for trial has not run and no motion for severance has been granted," is excludable in computing the time within which the trial of any offence must commence.)

10. Infra note 3; also see Rule 12 of the Federal Rules of Criminal Procedure.

11. 475 F Supp 903 (DC., 1979).

12. 408 US 665, 92 S Ct 2636 (1972). According to the majority opinion, the case (and two others decided together)

press First Amendment claims that may be simply put: that to gather news it is often necessary to agree either not to identify the source of information published or to publish only part of the facts revealed, or both; that if the reporter is nevertheless forced to reveal these confidences to a grand jury, the source so identified and other confidential sources of other reporters will be measurably deterred from furnishing publishable information, all to the detriment of the free flow of information protected by the First Amendment. Although petitioners do not claim an absolute privilege against official interrogation in all circumstances, they assert that the reporter should not be forced either to appear or to testify before a grand jury or at trial until and unless sufficient grounds are shown for believing that the reporter possesses information relevant to a crime the grand jury is investigating, that the information the reporter has is unavailable from other sources, and that the need for the information is sufficiently compelling to override the claimed invasion of First Amendment interests occasioned by the disclosure . . . The heart of the claim is that the burden on news gathering resulting from compelling reporters to disclose confidential information outweighs any public interest in obtaining the information.

[We agree] that news gathering [qualifies] for First Amendment protection; without some protection for seeking out the news, freedom of the press could be eviscerated. But this case involves no intrusions upon speech or assembly [and no] command that the press publish what it prefers to withhold. [N]o penalty, civil or criminal, related to the content of published material is at issue here. The use of confidential sources by the press is not forbidden or restricted; reporters remain free to seek news from any source by means within the law.

13. The Court concluded:

[T]he First Amendment does not guarantee the press a constitutional right of special access to information not available to the public generally. [Although] news gathering may be hampered, the press is regularly excluded from grand jury proceedings, our own conferences, the meetings of other official bodies gathered in executive session, and the meetings of private organizations. Newsmen have no constitutional right of access to the scenes of crime or disaster when the general public is excluded, and they may be prohibited from attending or publishing information about trials if such restrictions are necessary to assure a defendant a fair trial before an impartial tribunal. [It] is thus not surprising that the great weight of authority is that newsmen are not exempt from the normal duty of appearing before a grand jury and answering questions relevant to a criminal investigation. . . .

The prevailing constitutional view of the newsman's privilege is very much rooted in the ancient role of the grand jury which has the dual function of determining if there is probable cause to believe that a crime has been committed and of protecting citizens against unfounded criminal prosecutions. . . .

Because its task is to inquire into the existence of possible criminal conduct and to return only well-founded indictments, its investigative powers are necessarily broad. . . . Hence the grand jury's authority to subpoena witnesses is not only historic, but essential to its task. [T]he long standing principle that "the public has a right to every man's evidence," except for those persons protected by a constitutional, common law, or statutory privilege is particularly applicable to grand jury proceedings.

A [minority] of States have provided newsmen a statutory privilege of varying breadth, [but] none has been provided by federal statute. Until now the only [federal constitutional] testimonial privilege for unofficial witnesses [is] the Fifth Amendment privilege against compelled self-incrimination. We are asked to create another by interpreting the First Amendment to grant newsmen a testimonial privilege that other citizens do not enjoy. This we decline to do. [On] the records now before us, we perceive no basis for holding that the public interest in law enforcement and in ensuring effective grand jury proceedings is insufficient to override the consequential, but uncertain, burden on news gathering which is said to result from insisting that reporters, like other citizens, respond to relevant questions put to them in the course of a valid grand jury investigation or criminal trial.

This conclusion [does not] threaten the vast bulk of confidential relationships between reporters and their sources. Grand juries address themselves to the issues of whether crimes have been committed and who committed them. Only where news sources themselves are implicated in crime or possess information relevant to the grand jury's task need they or the reporter be concerned about grand jury subpoenas. Nothing before us indicates that a large number or percentage of *all* confidential news sources fall into either category and would in any way be deterred by our holding that the Constitution does not, as it never has, exempt the newsman from performing the citizen's normal duty of appearing and furnishing information relevant to the grand jury's task. . . .

There remain those situations where a source is not engaged in criminal conduct but has information suggesting illegal conduct by others. [The] argument that the flow of news will be diminished by compelling reporters to aid the grand jury in a criminal investigation is not irrational, nor are the records before us silent on the matter. But we remain unclear how often and to what extent informers are actually deterred from furnishing information when newsmen are forced to testify before a grand jury. . . .

We are admonished that refusal to provide a First Amendment reporter's privilege will undermine the freedom of the press to collect and disseminate news. But this is not the lesson history teaches us. [T]he common law recognized no such privilege, and the constitutional argument was not even asserted until 1958. From the beginning of our country the press has operated without constitutional protection for press informants, and the press has flourished. . . .

It is said that currently press subpoenas have multiplied, that mutual distrust and tension between press and officialdom have increased, that reporting styles have changed, and that there is now more need for confidential sources, particularly where the press seeks news about minority cultural and political groups or dissident organizations suspicious of the law and public officials. These developments, even if true, are treacherous grounds for a far-reaching interpretation of the First Amendment fastening a nationwide rule on courts, grand juries, and prosecuting officials everywhere. The obligation to testify in response to grand jury subpoenas will not threaten these sources not involved with criminal conduct and without information relevant to grand jury investigations, and we cannot hold that the Constitution places the sources in these two categories either above the law or beyond its reach.

The argument for such a constitutional privilege rests heavily on those cases holding that the infringement of protected First Amendment rights must be no broader than necessary to achieve a permissible governmental purpose. We do not deal, however, with a governmental institution that has abused its proper function, as a legislative committee does when it "expose[s] for the sake of exposure." [Nor is there any] attempt here by the grand juries to invade protected First Amendment rights by forcing wholesale disclosure of names and organizational affiliations for a purpose which is not germane to the determination of whether crime has been committed, and the characteristic secrecy of grand jury proceedings is a further protection against the undue invasion of such rights.

14. According to Justice Douglas,

two principles which follow from understanding of the First Amendment are at stake here. One is that the people, the ultimate governors, must have absolute freedom of and therefore privacy of their individual opinions and beliefs regardless of how suspect or strange they may appear to others. Ancillary to that principle is the conclusion that an individual must also have absolute privacy over whatever information he may generate in the course of testing his opinions and beliefs. In this regard, . . . status as a reporter is less relevant than is his status as a student who affirmatively pursued empirical research to enlarge his own intellectual viewpoint. The second principle is that effective self-government cannot succeed unless the people are immersed in a steady, robust, unimpeded, and uncensored flow of opinion and reporting which are continuously subjected to critique, rebutal, and re-examination. In this respect, status as a newsgatherer and an integral part of that process becomes critical. . . .

In recent years we have said over and again that where First Amendment rights are concerned any regulation "narrowly drawn," must be "compelling" and not merely "rational" as is the case where other activities are concerned. But the "compelling" interest in regulation neither includes paring down or diluting the right, nor embraces penalizing one solely for his intellectual viewpoint; it concerns the State's interest, for example, in regulating the time and place or perhaps manner of exercising First Amendment rights.

The dissent of Justice Stewart (joined in by Justices Brennan and Marshall) stated that

the Court's crabbed view of the First Amendment reflects a disturbing insensitivity to the critical role of an independent press in our society. The question whether a reporter has a constitutional right to a confidential relationship with his source is of first impression here, but the principles which should guide our decision are as basic as any to be found in the Constitution. While Mr. Justice Powell's enigmatic concurring opinion gives some hope of a more flexible view in the future, the Court in these cases holds that a newsman has no First Amendment right to protect his sources when called before a grand jury. The Court thus invites state and federal authorities to undermine the historic independence of the press by attempting to annex the journalistic profession as an investigative arm of government. Not only will this decision impair performance of the press' constitutionally protected functions, but it will, I am convinced, in the long run, harm rather than help the administration of justice. . . . As private and public aggregations of power burgeon in size and the pressures for conformity necessarily mount, there is obviously a continuing need for an independent press to disseminate a robust variety of information and opinion through reportage, investigation and criticism, if we are to preserve our constitutional tradition of maximizing freedom of choice by encouraging diversity of expression. . . .

[W]hen an investigation impinges on First Amendment rights, the government must not only show that the inquiry is of "compelling and overriding importance" but it must also "convincingly" demonstrate that the investigation is "substantially related" to the information sought. Governmental officials must, therefore, demonstrate that the information sought is *clearly* relevant to a *precisely* defined subject of governmental inquiry. They must demonstrate that it is reasonable to think the witness in question has that information. And they must show that there is not any means of obtaining the information less destructive of First Amendment liberties. . . .

I believe the safeguards developed in our decisions involving governmental investigations must apply to the grand jury inquiries in these cases. Surely the function of the grand jury to aid in the enforcement of the law is no more important than the function of the legislature, and its committees, to make the law. . . . Similarly, the associational rights of private individuals, which have been the prime focus of our First Amendment decisions in the investigative sphere, are hardly more important than the First Amendment rights of mass circulation newspapers and electronic media to disseminate ideas and information, and of the general public to receive them. Moreover, the vices of vagueness and overbreadth which legislative investigations may manifest are also exhibited by grand jury inquiries, since grand jury investigations are not limited in scope to specific criminal acts.

15. ____F2d____ (2nd Cir., Nov. 25, 1987).

16. Citing Brady v. Maryland, 373 US 83 (1963), the court pointed out that the U.S. Supreme Court in that case had held that the "suppression by the prosecution of evidence favorable to an accused upon request violates due process where the evidence is material either to guilt or to punishment" (373 U.S. at 87). As a threshold matter, the defendant must show that the government actually suppressed evidence. Since the prosecutor's duty to disclose necessarily extends only to "information which had been known to the prosecution but unknown to the defense (*United States v. Agurs*, 427 U.S. 97, 103 [1976]), evidence is not suppressed and *Brady* is not applicable where the defendant either knew or should have known the essential facts permitting him to take advantage of the evidence in question. See *United States v. Gaggi*, 811 F. 2d 47, 59 (2d Cir.) *cert denied*, 107 S. Ct. 3214 (1987); *United States v. LeRoy*, 687 F. 2d 610, 618 (2d Cir. 1982), *cert. denied*, 459 U.S. 1174 (1983); *United States v. Prior*, 546 F. 2d 1254, 1259 (5th Cir. 1977). That is this case."

17. ____NY 2d____, ____NE 2d____ (December 24, 1987).

18. ____F2d____ (2nd Cir., January 15, 1988).

19. ____AD2d____, ____NYS2d____ (January 11, 1988).

20. See Vorenberg, "Decent Restraint of Prosecutorial Power," 94 Harv L Rev 1521 (May 1981).

21. Id. at 1523:

To be sure, the divergence between our stated ideal for criminal justice and the actual operation of that system should not be overstated. The ultimate protection for one accused of crime is his "day in court," the confrontation with his accuser. The accused's freedom is guaranteed unless the state can convince a judge or jury of his guilt beyond a reasonable doubt. The drama of a criminal trial has a strong hold on public imagination, but what happens in court is not theater; it is the core of a system of justice that aims to protect the innocent from the consequences of a false conviction, and the innocent and guilty alike from affronts to their dignity. The trial is open to the public both to protect the defendant against prejudice and abuse and to serve the public's interest in knowing how officials deal with those accused of crime.

22. See Newman v. United States, 382 F2d 479 (DC Cir., 1967) at 480.

23. 118 US 356 (1886).

24. See United States v. Nixon, 418 US 683 (1974), and Oyler v. Boles, 368 US 448 (1962).

25. See generally 94 Harv L Rev 887 (1981).

26. Note 18 USC 1503 (1976).

27. See Wigmore, Evidence, Section 940 (rev ed., 1970).
28. See such decisions as Annunziato v. Manson, 556 F2d 410 (2nd Cir., 1977), Giglio v. United States, 405 US 150 (1972), United States v. Jackson, 579 F2d 553 (10th Cir., 1978).
29. Infra note 23 at 889.
30. See United States v. Sutton, 542 F2d 1239 (4th Cir., 1979).
31. 427 US 97 (1976).
32. Infra note 23 at 892.
33. See Alcorta v. Texas, 355 US 28 (1957) at 31.
34. See U.S. v. McClintic, 570 F2d 685 (8th Cir., 1978) at 692:

Rudimentary demands of a fair trial also require that the terms of a plea bargain reached with a material prosecution witness be disclosed to the judge and jury so that the trier of fact may weigh the witness' credibility. . . . While this doctrine arose from a series of cases in which witnesses were allowed to perjure themselves as to agreements made, either through inadvertance or design, it also encompasses situations in which the government allows materially misleading statements to go uncorrected.

35. _____NYS 2d_____ (AD1, December 15, 1987).
36. See United States v. Monks, 774 F2d 945 (9th Cir., 1985).
37. See Snow v. Reid, 619 F Supp 579 (SDNY, 1985).
38. 784 F2d 1093 (11th Cir., 1986).
39. 705 P2d 130 (Nev., 1985).
40. 804 F2d 210 (2nd Cir., 1986). Note People v. Gilmore, NYS2d (ad2, January 7, 1988) where the New York Appellate Division, 2nd Dept., affirmed a judgment of conviction:

We find unpersuasive the defendant's contention that he was denied a fair trial due to several remarks made by the prosecutor in his closing statements. Although these remarks may have been improper, any objections asserted were sustained and the court promptly issued curative instructions which were sufficient to dispel whatever prejudicial effect those remarks may had held (see, People v. Jones, 120 AD 2d 747; People v. Walters, 116 AD 2d 757, 1v denied 67 NY 2d 891). Moreover, the cumulative effect of the comments was not so prejudicial as to have compromised the defendant's right to a fair trial (see, People v. Roopchand, 107 AD 2d 35, affd NY 2d 837).

41. 803 F2d 1969 (9th Cir., 1986).
42. 801 F2d 1543 (9th Cir., 1986).
43. 106 S Ct 2464 (1986).
44. See generally *Trial Magazine* (September 1987) at 55 et seq.
45. _____F2d_____ (2nd Cir., February 26, 1988).
46. Note the reasoning of the court in evaluating the two sides:

the government argues that an order denying a motion to dismiss an indictment for alleged grand jury abuses does not qualify as a final decision under the collateral order doctrine and, therefore, is not subject to interlocutory review. The Supreme Court has noted that adherence to the rule of finality is particularly important in criminal cases, "because 'the delays and disruptions attendant upon intermediate appeal,' which the rule is designed to avoid, 'are especially inimical to the effective and fair administration of the criminal law.' " *Abney v. United States*, 431 U.S. 651, 657 (1977) (quoting *DiBella v. United States*, 369 U.S. 121, 126 (1962)). Delay in criminal cases infringes not only upon the defendant's interest in the speedy resolution of charges against him, but also upon society's interest in the prompt administration of justice. Over time, the prosecution's ability to prove its case diminishes as evidence deteriorates and witnesses' memories fade; society may be forced to bear the cost of extended pretrial detention or, alternatively, to assume the risk that defendants released pending trial may commit other crimes. Flanagan v. United States, 465 U.S. 259, 264–65 (1984). With these concerns in mind, the Supreme Court thus far has recognized the following types of pretrial orders in criminal cases that meet the requirements of the collateral order exception: an order denying a motion for reduction of bail, *Stack v. Boyle*, 342 U.S. 1 (1951); an order denying a motion to dismiss an indictment where it is claimed it violates the double jeopardy clause, *Abney*, 431 U.S. 651; and an order denying a motion to dismiss an indictment on the ground that it violates the speech and debate clause, *Helstoski v. Meanor*, 442 U.S. 500 (1979). Apart from these exceptions, the general rule is that an order denying a motion to dismiss an indictment is interlocutory and not appealable. *United States v. Beckerman*, 516 F.2d 905, 906 (2d Cir. 1975). See also United States Tour Operators Ass'n v. Trans World Airlines, 556 F.2d 128 (2d Cir.1977) (stating that "Attempts to come within the scope of the *Cohen* doctrine have been legion, but we have not been receptive to an expansive reading of this exception to the final judgment rule.").

Respondents argue, however, that in light of the Supreme Court's decision in *United States v. Mechanik*, 475 U.S. 66 (1986), the denial of their motions to dismiss the indictment is effectively unreviewable following the conclusion of trial, and therefore should be subject to interlocutory review. Respondents argue that, if they are acquitted, the denial of their motions to dismiss will be moot; however, if they are convicted, the grand jury abuses of which they complain will be deemed harmless error under *Mechanik*, and thus insufficient to warrant reversing the convictions. Respondents find support for this argument in the dissenting opinion in *Mechanik*, 475 U.S. at 81 n.1 (Marshall, J., dissenting), as well as in two circuit court cases, *see United States v. Dederich*, 825 F.2d 1317 (9th Cir. 1987); *United States v. Benjamin*, 812 F.2d 548 (9th Cir. 1987). At least two other circuits, however, have reached the opposite conclusion. *See United States v. LaRouche Campaign*, 829 F.2d 250 (1st Cir. 1987); *United States v. Taylor*, 798 F.2d 1337 (10th Cir. 1986).

47. See Hawthorne v. United States, 476 A2d 164 (DC App., 1984); State v. Couture, 482 A2d 300 (Conn., 1984), cert den 105 S Ct 967 (1985); State v. Anderson, 718 P2d 400 (Utah, 1986); State v. Wheeler, 468 So2d 978 (Fla., 1985); Good v. State, 723 SW2d 734 (Tex Crim App., 1986); and Bertolotti v. State, 476 So2d 130 (Fla., 1985).

48. See ABAJ (October 1, 1987) at 46 et seq.

49. 100 US 371 (1880).

50. See 94 Harv L Rev 1244 (1981) at 1373 et seq and at 1413 et seq.

51. Id. at 1414.
52. Note ABA Standards for Criminal Justice, Standard 3-1.1(b) (1980).
53. See generally 128 U Pa L Rev 733 (1980), and 29 Syracuse L Rev 697 (1978).
54. See United States v. Birdman, 602 F2d 547 (3rd Cir., 1979), cert den 444 US 1032 (1980).
55. Infra note 46 at 1422 to 1428.

9

Criminal Procedure and the Fair and Speedy Trial

9.1 JURISDICTION GENERALLY

Jurisdiction over criminal offenses means the power of a given court to inquire into and determine whether or not an alleged criminal offense has been committed by a designated accused person or persons, and to apply the penalty of an offense so determined.[1] This definition of criminal jurisdiction embraces, it is said, certain principles: (a) the jurisdiction of any court varies with its position in the hierarchy of tribunals, from trial courts to appellate courts; (b) the jurisdiction of a court may be limited by the character of the offense committed, i.e., the minor offenses are tried in the lowest court which would not have jurisdiction over the serious, capital offenses; (c) the character of the penalty to be imposed may restrict the jurisdiction of the court, or the jurisdiction may be circumscribed by the penalty to be imposed; (d) the territory where the offense was committed limits jurisdiction, in the sense that a city court cannot try an offense committed outside the city, unless a change of venue has been legally secured; (e) the personality of the government may determine jurisdiction, although an offense against federal law may still be cognizable in state courts, and offenses against foreign governments may be tried in either federal or state courts; (f) the character of the accused may determine jurisdiction as where the offender is a juvenile; (g) statutes of limitations may bar jurisdiction; (h) the repeal of a criminal statute may oust a court of jurisdiction; (i) the assumption of jurisdiction by one court may bar another court from exercising jurisdiction over the same offense; (j) the presence or absence of the offender may determine jurisdiction, for the criminal accused must be present in court at the time he is being tried; (k) the citizenship of the offender may limit a court's jurisdiction, particularly where the offender is, or is employed by, a foreign sovereign, and the law of the foreign sovereign may be applicable until the offender comes within the jurisdiction of the non-foreign court; but persons who are citizens of no country will be subject to the jurisdiction of the courts of all sovereigns. Indeed, the locus of the offense fixes jurisdiction, but the dictates of a fair and speedy trial may change the venue, as illustrated by the Pennsylvania Supreme Court in Commonwealth v. Baltz[2]: "In this country and England, the common law right of trial by jury of the county or vicinage was not unconditional, but the trial might be removed to another county upon application of either the Crown, the prosecution, or the accused when it was thought to be necessary to assure a 'fair and impartial trial.' "[3]

9.2 PREVENTATIVE DETENTION AND THE BAIL REFORM ACT OF 1984

The procedure of bail was designed to keep the criminal defendant within the jurisdiction of the court prior to and during the trial. But the bail system has not facilitated the subsequent criminal trial, especially with the cudgel of the Eighth Amendment against excessive bail[4] swinging over the prosecution and the judiciary. In People ex rel Benton v. Wharton[5] the New York court in 1986 stated that "presumption of innocence accorded every criminal defendant militates strongly against incarceration in advance of determination as to guilt." Here a $25,000 bail set by the arraigning judge was struck down in light of the fact that the defendant was present in all of his prior appearances. It should be noted that the Eighth Amendment protection afforded the criminal defendant has been consistently applied to the states.[6] Most recently, the New York Appellate Division refused to allow a court to increase a defendant's bail beyond the amount originally set without proof by the prosecution of changed circumstances warranting increased bail.[7] The New York Criminal Procedural Law delineates the following factors that a court must take into consideration in setting bail: (a) the principal's character, reputation, habits, and mental condition; (b) his/her employment and financial resources; (c) his/her family ties and length of present residence; (d) his/her criminal record, if any; (e) his/her record of previous adjudication as juvenile delinquent or youthful offender; (f) his/her previous record in responding to court appearances when required or with respect to flight to avoid criminal prosecution; (g) evidence against him/her in the pending criminal actions, and the probability of conviction; and (h) the likely sentence that may be imposed upon him/her.[8]

The Bail Reform Act of 1984[9] authorizes federal judicial officers to detain a criminal defendant before trial if the federal judicial officer determines that the defendant is likely to commit a crime while on release, pending trial. The Act allows the federal court to detain the arrested person if the federal government can demonstrate by clear and convincing evidence, after an adversary hearing, that the "no release" condition "will reasonably assure . . . the safety of any other person and the community."[10] In Salerno v. United States[11] the U.S. Supreme Court observed that the criminal defendant, charged with a RICO violation, had been detained for more than fourteen months,[12] and that the Second U.S. Court of Appeals had struck the preventative detention provision as a violation of "substantive due process."[13] The highest court reversed, holding the Act constitutional and pointing out that under the Act the federal courts may jail criminal defendants before trial if the criminal defendants are deemed a threat to public safety. The 6-3 opinion written by Chief Justice Rehnquist emphasized that the federal court did not have free rein in making a preventative detention decision, for Congress under the Act required the federal judicial officer to consider the nature and seriousness of the charges, the substantiality of the evidence against the criminal defendant, the defendant's background and characteristics, and the nature and seriousness of the danger to the safety of the public posed by the defendant's release. There was no violation of substantive due process, for mere detention is not equal to punishment: "Preventing danger to the community is a legitimate regulatory goal."[14] Thus, the highest court put its stamp of approval upon "safety of the community" as an additional reason for preventative detention when the avowed constitutional purpose was simply to assure the defendant's presence in the courtroom where he would enjoy his right to a fair and speedy trial.[15]

Indeed, prior to the enactment of the Act, judicial officers could consider only the risk of flight of the criminal defendant in determining bail in non-capital cases.[16]

The detention hearing itself places the burden of proof upon the federal government; the defendant has the right to be represented by counsel, to testify in his own behalf, to present witnesses, and to cross-examine the government's witnesses. The determination of detention must be based upon "probable cause" and the charged offense must prescribe a "maximum term of imprisonment of ten years or more."[17] Once the judicial officer makes a finding, a rebuttable presumption is triggered that "no condition or combination of conditions of release will reasonably assure the appearance of the person as required and the safety of the community."[18] The Second U.S. Court of Appeals in its 1986 decision in United States v. Melendez-Carrion[19] held that preventative detention was inconsistent with the traditions of our constitutional system of criminal justice because "detention to prevent the commission of domestic crime can constitutionally occur only after conviction." Furthermore, preventative detention cannot be upheld simply because it is a rational means of promoting public safety. Professor Lawrence Tribe of Harvard Law School took the position that detaining an individual "capable of conforming to society's demands" is a peculiarly "offensive anticipatory condemnation" that is inconsistent with constitutional traditions.[20]

9.3 PROCEDURAL RIGHTS IN FEDERAL MAGISTRATE COURTS

Misdemeanors committed within federal jurisdiction have since 1979 been tried before United States magistrates,[21] and the rules of procedure and practice for the trial of cases in federal magistrate courts were adopted by the U.S. Supreme Court.[22] At first, no right to jury trial existed where the defendant elected to be tried before a federal magistrate; indeed, the election constituted a waiver of the right to a jury trial.[23] But in 1979 Congress amended the Federal Magistrate Act,[24] and the guarantees of the Sixth Amendment were made applicable to "misdemeanors" as distinguished from "petty offenses." The procedural safeguards of the Federal Rules of Criminal Procedure, including the right to counsel and jury trial,[25] are applicable in "all proceedings except those concerning petty offenses for which no sentence of imprisonment will be imposed."[26] The federal magistrate was thus enabled to conduct jury trials and expand his/her ability to try most misdemeanor cases.

The Assimilative Crimes Act[27] provides for punishment by creating a federal offense with reference to state law for its definition and penalty. The procedural guarantees are, nevertheless, applicable, as indicated in Smayda v. United States,[28] to wit: a defendant prosecuted for commission of a state misdemeanor which occurs on federally owned or federally controlled property is entitled to the rights provided by federal constitutional law and criminal procedure. Indeed, the U.S. Supreme Court in Duncan v. Louisiana[29] established the rule that the Fourteenth Amendment embraces the right to a jury trial in state offenses to the same extent as provided under federal law.

9.4 THE SPEEDY TRIAL AND THE PROSECUTOR'S UNAVAILABILITY

The criminal defendant's right to a speedy trial may be jeopardized by the prosecutor's unavailability, as delineated in People v. Weigand-Gordon.[30] Here the criminal action against the defendant was commenced in October 1985 by the issuance and filing of a felony complaint and the issuance of an arrest warrant. About eighteen months later defendant moved to dismiss the indictment on the grounds that her right to a speedy trial had been denied. The prosecution contended that, while the New York statute required the prosecution to be ready for trial within six months of the commencement of the criminal action, there was "more than enough excludable time" that the motion to dismiss must be denied. It appears that the prosecutor within the six-month period of time had been in a serious automobile accident and had been hospitalized with about one hundred stitches to her head. She had been in this case since December 1985 and "was deeply involved in its investigation and the arraignment. The subject matter of this action is unique in a sense. It involved the alleged crimes of forgery and unauthorized practice of medicine which are subjects not frequently handled by other Assistant Attorney Generals."[31] Accordingly, the court ruled that, although a prosecutor's illness is not an excuse for delay, the "extraordinary circumstances" precluded penalizing the prosecution, and the defendant's motion to dismiss was denied.

In a similar vein is People v. Ralim Bey-Allah[32] where the criminal defendant was not given notice by the prosecutor of the grand jury proceeding, even though he had served the prosecutor with timely notice as required by statute of his intention to appear and testify before the grand jury. But here the New York appellate court reversed the conviction; the defendant was prejudiced by not being given a reasonable time to exercise his right to appear before the grand jury which indicted him. Defendant was in effect denied his right to a speedy trial and also his right to a fair trial: "The prejudice is obvious, since it results from the fact that the defendant will be testifying before a grand jury that has already been instructed on the law, discussed the case among themselves, and voted to indict the defendant."

9.5 INCRIMINATING STATEMENTS OF THE DEFENDANT

Incriminating statements of the criminal defendant were carefully examined in the 1964 decision of the U.S. Supreme Court in Massiah v. United States,[33] and the highest court there reversed the conviction of the defendant, who, having been arrested and released on bail after retaining counsel, gave incriminating statements to his "friend" who was a cooperating informant secretly recording their conversations. Five years earlier in People of the State of New York v. Spano[34] the Court had held it constitutionally impermissible, under certain circumstances, for federal government agents to surreptitiously obtain incriminating statements from a defendant after the defendant is arraigned on criminal charges and either placed in custody or released on bail. The "friend scenario," nevertheless, is apparently still utilized by the prosecution, but under greater discipline and at times *before* indictment. The federal district court for the Eastern District of New York in United States v. Hammad[35] in 1987, however, precluded the prosecution from permitting cooperating informants to tape-record witnesses or putative defendants who are represented by counsel; and the court suppressed the recordings containing the incriminating statements. The court's ruling was not premised on the Sixth Amendment's guarantees (which constitutional grounds do not attach during the pre-indictment stage),[36] nor on the Fourteenth Amendment's due process of law clause;[37] its ruling was based on the disciplinary rule violations under DR 7–104(A)(1) by the prosecutor. The court expressly found that the prosecutor was in fact aware of the tape recording before it was conducted, and therefore suppression of that evidence was warranted, not only for the disciplinary rule violation, but in the interests of a fair trial for the criminal defendant. But on December 10, 1987, in United States v. Guerrerio[38] the federal District Court for the Southern District of New York denied the defendant's suppression motion based on DR7–104(A)(1); that court found that the suppression remedy against the incriminating statement made by the defendant during the pre-arrest stage of the criminal proceedings was not necessary because the prosecutor's conduct here did not constitute a disciplinary rule violation in the first place. That court opined that the disciplinary rule only prohibits "communication with a party known to be represented by an attorney" and a grand jury witness is not a "party" since he or she is not yet a "party" to a prosecution.

9.6 "DOUBLE JEOPARDY"

The "double jeopardy" scenario, possibly impinging also upon the defendant's right to a fair trial, was in evidence in the recent New York Court of Appeal's decision in In the Matter of Kaplan v. Ritter.[39] The petitioners, who had been convicted in the federal court of various conspiracy and fraud counts, sought a New York court order to prohibit the New York City prosecutor from trying them on charges of larceny and securities fraud arising from the same transaction. The highest New York court sensed the "double jeopardy" and declared:

Their appeal . . . requires us to consider the scope and proper application of CPL 40.20(2)(e) which establishes an exception to the general statutory rules against successive prosecutions where "each offense involves death, injury, loss or other consequences to a different victim." We hold that this exception is available only where each of the offenses in the separate prosecutions involves one or more specific, individually identifiable victims. Accordingly, where, as here, the accused have been previously tried and convicted on federal conspiracy, racketeering, and fraud charges, all of which were based on a bribery scheme having no identifiable victims, the "different victim" exception of CPL 40.20(2)(e) cannot be invoked to justify a separate prosecution for State larceny and securities fraud arising from the same bribery scheme. . . . We conclude that the exception provided in CPL 40.20(2)(e) for offenses involving different victims has no application in this situation. . . . To permit application of the CPL 40.20(2)(e) "different victim" exception in these circumstances would be to distort the carefully crafted statutory double jeopardy scheme.''[40]

The court concluded: "In light of our decision on the proper application of the statutory double jeopardy provisions, we need not consider petitioners' other arguments addressed to the State and federal constitutional proscriptions (U.S. Const., Amends V and XIV; N.Y. Const., Art. 1, Sec. 6)."

9.7 THE DEFENSE OF MISTAKE OF LAW

The defense of mistake of law was held by New York's highest court in People v. Marrero[41] not to be available to a federal corrections officer (from Danbury, Connecticut) arrested in 1977 in a New York City social club for possession of a loaded .380 automatic pistol. The criminal defendant claimed that he mistakingly believed that he was entitled to carry a handgun without a permit as a peace officer. The trial court had rejected his defense, and he was convicted of criminal possession of a weapon in the third degree. According to the court, the common law rule on mistake of law meant that the defendant could not be relieved of criminal liability, i.e., ignorance of the law is no excuse. Section 265.20 of the New York Penal Law[42] and Section 2.10 of the New York Civil Practice Law fortify this conclusion:[43] "The defense should not be recognized, except where specific intent is an element of the offense or where the misrelied-upon law has later been properly adjudicated as wrong.''[44] The New York Court of Appeals concluded:

Strong public policy reasons underlie the legislative mandate and intent which we perceive in rejecting defendant's construction of New York's mistake of law defense statute. If defendant's argument were accepted, the exception would swallow the rule. Mistakes about the law would be encouraged, rather than respect for and adherence to law. There would be an infinite number of mistake of law defenses which could be devised from a good faith, perhaps reasonable but mistaken, interpretation of criminal statutes, many of which are concededly complex. Even more troublesome are the opportunities for wrong-minded individuals to contrive in bad faith solely to get an exculpatory notion before the jury.[45]

The dissent of Judge Hancock maintained that rejection of the defense of mistake of law was "directly contrary to the plain dictates of the statute and a rejection of the jurisprudential reforms and legislative policies underlying its enactment."[46]

9.8 IDENTIFICATION OF THE DEFENDANT

A fair trial may mandate proper identification of the defendant. In United States v. Sabater[47] the Second U.S. Court of Appeals affirmed the conviction of a woman accused of selling "crack" to an under-cover officer. At the trial the officer who bought the narcotic testified, and during this examination the defendant sat at the defense table wearing a blue-striped blazer. On cross-examination, the officer was asked by the defense to identify the defendant and he pointed to the woman at the defense table. But, unbeknown to the court, jury, and the prose-cution, the defense attorney had substituted defendant's sister wearing the same blue-striped blazer. The trial court immediately called a re-cess, castigated defense counsel for the "trick," and then ordered both sisters to sit at the defense table, whereupon the officer correctly iden-tified the defendant. The "switch" was unnecessary, according to the court, because defense counsel could have moved for a lineup to as-sure correct identification, or have people of the defendant's proximate age and skin color sit near her. In either event, defendant received a fair trial, for the officer saw the defendant for "a few seconds" when he bought the "crack" from her, saw her again when she was ar-rested, and observed her the third time at the police station, thus "making his identification (of her) sufficiently reliable."

9.9 MOTION FOR CONTINUANCE

The defense in the criminal trial utilizes the motion for continuance to maintain the fair trial standard when defense requires more time to prepare for trial.[48] The motion for continuance may relate to the need for more time to secure the presence of new or unavailable wit-nesses.[49] The Eleventh U.S. Court of Appeals in United States v. Darby[50] described the prerequisite for a successful motion for contin-uance: "Movant must show . . . that due diligence has been exer-cised to obtain the attendance of the witness, that substantial favorable evidence would be tendered by the witness, that the witness is avail-able and willing to testify, and that the denial of continuance would materially prejudice the defendant."[51] Where the prosecution has made inadequate pre-trial disclosure of material evidence, or where the government has interfered with defendant's right to effective assistance of counsel, the motion for continuance should readily be granted.[52]

Basically, the decision to grant or deny a continuance rests within the sound discretion of the trial court, as set forth by the U.S. Supreme Court in Ungar v. Sarafite.[53] But courts must exercise care to avoid undue interference with fundamental rights of the criminal defendant under the Sixth Amendment and the Fourteenth Amendment.[54] Factors such as timeliness of the motion for continuance,[55] the actual amount of time defense counsel had to prepare the case,[56] and likelihood that continuance would aid one party at the expense of the other,[57] will weigh heavily in the court's discretion.

9.10 FREEZING OR FORFEITURE OF DEFENDANT'S ASSETS

The freezing or forfeiture of criminal defendant's assets are possible under several federal statutes, and the consequences pose a serious threat to the rights of the defendant to a fair and speedy trial. For example, under the Comprehensive Forfeiture Act of 1970,[58] all property or proceeds derived from drug or organized crime violations are forfeitable to the federal government. Until 1984 and before indictment the defendant had the right to transfer irrevocably those assets which the government had not seized. But frequently those assets were simply not available to pay attorneys' fees, and therefore the criminal defendant was deprived of his choice of counsel. The Comprehensive Crime Control Act of 1984 provides that forfeiture relates back to the commission of the act giving rise to forfeiture.[59] Thus, any forfeitable property transferred to another person after commission of the crime is also forfeited to the government "unless the transferee establishes in a post-trial hearing . . . that he is a bona fide purchaser for value" and that he was at the time of the purchase "reasonably without cause to believe that the property was subject to forfeiture."[60]

The U.S. Justice Department Guidelines on Forfeiture of Attorneys' Fees[61] takes the unusual step of sanctioning the forfeiture of attorneys' fees if the fees were "paid from assets that are forfeitable." In effect, the attorney for the criminal defendant has a "contingency fee" arrangement,[62] contrary to Rule 1.5(d)(2) of the ABA Model Rules of Professional Conduct.[63]

As the federal district court expressed it,

No one is more on notice of the likelihood that the money may come from . . . prohibited activity than the lawyer who is asked to represent the defendant in the trial of the indictment. If the statute applies to him, its message to him is "Do not represent this defendant or you will lose your fee." . . . By the Sixth Amendment we guarantee the defendant the right of counsel, but by the forfeiture provisions . . . we insure that no lawyer will accept the business.[64]

As exemplified in United States v. Reckmeyer,[65] there is also a conflict of interest between the lawyer and his client, to wit: the lawyer's "obligation to negotiate a guilty plea which is in his client's best interest may conflict with his desire to have his client enter a plea that does not involve forfeiture" of the client's assets from which the attorney's fee will be paid. Indeed, the right to counsel belonging to the criminal defendant may be infringed, but the U.S. Supreme Court in 1932 declared that the right to counsel of choice is only a qualified right.[66] In United States v. Ianniello[67] it was held that bona fide attorneys' fees were not intended to be forfeitable. The Fourth U.S. Court of Appeals in 1987 in United States v. Harvey[68] ruled that the forfeiture provisions violated the defendant's qualified right to counsel of choice, despite the government's valid interests in preserving the availability of the defendant's assets for forfeiture, in stripping racketeers and drug dealers of their economic power upon conviction, and in deterring the commission of crime.[69] In United States v. Monsanto[70] the Second U.S. Court of Appeals discussed the December 21, 1987 amendment to the Comprehensive Crime Control Act[71] on the federal government's power before trial to obtain an ex parte order freezing assets that defendants in a criminal case might use to pay their attorneys' fees. The federal appellate court here mandated a hearing at which the federal government must prove the "probability" that the defendant will be convicted and that therefore the assets would be subject to seizure. Should defendant win this hearing, then any assets used to pay attorneys' fees would be exempt from post-trial forfeiture. (The dissenting opinion asserted that the provisions for forfeiture of defendant's assets were unconstitutional on both Sixth Amendment and on Fifth Amendment due process grounds.)

An interesting variation on this theme of protecting attorneys' fees derived from assets of the criminal defendant occured in People v. Winkler.[72] Here the defendant appealed his conviction for the murder of his father not only on the ground of ineffective assistance by counsel[73] but also on the ground that counsel had insisted upon a contingency fee arrangement under which he would receive an additional fee of $25,000 if the defendant were acquitted, or found not guilty by reason of insanity, or some other reason which would permit defendant to inherit from his slain father.[74] The New York Appellate Division, 2nd Dept., promptly vacated his conviction and ordered a new trial:

> We find that the instant retainer agreement is unethical as it is in violation of the Code of Professional Responsibility. Specifically DR 2-106(c) provides "a lawyer shall not enter into an arrangement for, charge or collect a contingent fee for representing a client in a criminal case." . . . In sum, we find that once a defendant establishes that a contingency fee arrangement, such as that at the bar, exists between himself or herself and defense counsel, the defendant has met the standard of demonstrating the existence of conflict or a significant possibility thereof . . . In any event, we conclude that in this case, as a matter of law, the defendant was denied his constitutional right to counsel . . . and the judgment of conviction [should be] vacated and a new trial ordered.[75]

The court also observed that EC 2-20 of the Code of Professional Responsibility similarly states that "public policy properly condemns contingent fee arrangements in criminal cases largely on the ground that legal services in criminal cases do not provide a *res* in which to pay the fee"; and moreover "this prohibition is further recognition of the fact that contingency fees, particularly in criminal cases, present an inherent danger of corrupting justice."[76] The court concluded that "given the unique conflict of interest arising in the contingency fee cases of this nature, reversal is necessary."[77]

The issue of freezing or forfeiture of a defendant's assets has also arisen in state court criminal proceedings, as illustrated by State of Connecticut v. Champagne.[78] The defendant businessman was accused of car theft; and when the state froze his assets before conviction, he argued that his constitutional right to an attorney was violated.

The prosecution contended that the criminal defendant did not have a constitutional right to a lawyer of his choosing; according to the prosecution brief, the founding fathers did not believe that a person should be able to rob a bank and then use the stolen money to hire the most expensive lawyer the criminal could find![79] The Connecticut Supreme Court in March 1988 ruled that the defendant could not prevail on his claim that the forfeiture and pre-trial freeze provisions of the Connecticut Corrupt Organizations and Racketeering Activity Act, or CORA, do not, without proof of intent to avoid forfeiture, reach property that was, like that in question here, transferred prior to the commencement of a CORA prosecution; bona fide pre-prosecution transfers are not per se exempt from forfeiture.[80] But defendant was entitled to an exemption for the interest component of the mortgage payments under CORA provision that exempts the net income or profits from property subject to forfeiture pending a final judgment of forfeiture. The court spelled out its reasoning:

The defendant argues broadly that the forfeiture and pretrial freeze provisions of CORA do not reach property that was transferred prior to the commencement of the prosecution unless the state proves that the transfer was made "with the intention of preventing its forfeiture" as specified under General Statutes §53-397(b)(3). Under that section, "the court may set aside" the fraudulent transfer and render appropriate orders "reasonably necessary to protect the rights of any innocent party to any such transfer." This claim of an implied limitation on CORA's reach finds support, according to the defendant, in the lack of any CORA provision relating the occurrence of forfeiture back to the time the offense was committed.

The state maintains, to the contrary, that the forfeitable property in this case, the purchase money mortgage on the Island Brook property, falls within the direct purview of forfeitures authorized by CORA. CORA authorizes forfeiture of "[a]ny property . . . acquired, maintained or used in violation of this chapter, including profits derived therefrom and the appreciated value thereof, or, where applicable, the proceeds from the sale thereof." (Emphasis added.) General Statutes §53-397 (a)(1). CORA defines "property" as "any property, real or personal, or any interest therein or any beneficial interest of whatever kind." General Statutes §53-394(g). According to the state, the set aside provision of §53-397(b)(3) upon which the defendant relies is an unrelated remedy that comes into play only when the "proceeds from the sale thereof" are patently insufficient in relation to the value of the property that was previously transferred.

The issue before us, therefore, is whether, in light of CORA's language and purpose, its forfeiture provisions encompass the defendant's mortgage payments as "proceeds from the sale" of real and personal property that was "acquired, maintained or used" in the commission of illegal racketeering activity. In our construction of the applicable statutory language, our goal is to "ascertain and give effect to the apparent intent of the legislature." *State v. Blasko*, 202 Conn. 541, 553, 522 A.2d 753 (1987). In reaching this goal, we consider first whether the language of the statute yields a plain and unambiguous resolution. *Rhodes v. Hartford*, 201 Conn. 89, 93, 513 A.2d 124(1986). Any latent ambiguity in the statutory language itself is normally resolved by turning for guidance to the legislative history and the purpose the statute is to serve. *State v. Kozlowski*, 199 Conn. 667, 673, 509 A.2d 20 (1986).

The defendant in this case urges us to apply a further maxim of statutory construction: the criminal sanction of forfeiture must be strictly construed. In support of this claim, the defendant asserts that the penalty of forfeiture is "foreign" to our law. In the unqualified form in which this assertion is stated, it is inaccurate. Recourse to forfeiture in certain cases is an ancient, albeit sparingly used, fixture in our criminal jurisprudence, as a brief review of the historical record demonstrates.

The common law of England recognized two principal types of forfeiture. The value of an object, or the object itself, that caused the accidental death of a King's subject was forfeited to the Crown as a deodand. J. Finkelstein, "The Goring Ox: Some Historical Perspectives on Deodands, Forfeitures, Wrongful Death and the Western Notion of Sovereignty," 46 Temp. L.Q. 169, 197 (1973). The common law also imposed a forfeiture of estate consequent to conviction of a felony or treason. Note, "Bane of American Forfeiture Law-Banished At Last?" 62 Cornell L. Rev. 768, 771–72 (1977). This latter penalty had two especially harsh results: the accused was deemed to forfeit the entirety of his personal and real property upon a judgment of conviction; *Calero-Toledo v. Pearson Yacht Leasing Co.*, 416 U.S. 663, 680–82, 94 S. Ct. 2080, 40 L. Ed. 2D 452 (1974); and his " 'blood was corrupted' so that nothing could pass by inheritance through his line." *United States v. Grande*, 620 F.2d 1026, 1038 (4th Cir.), cert. Denied sub nom. *Castagna v. United States*, 449 U.S. 830, 101 S. Ct. 98, 66 L. Ed. 2D 35 (1980).

Neither type of forfeiture gained currency in this country. The deodand was rejected largely because it was viewed as a superstitious institution that rested on a fiction that the offending object itself was morally afflicted for having caused death. *Parker-Harris Co. v. Tate*, 135 Tenn. 509, 514–15, 188 S.W. 54 (1916). The broad penalty of forfeiture of estate was also repudiated in Connecticut by the end of the eighteenth century. 2 Z. Swift, A System of the Laws of the State of Connecticut (1796) p. 405; see also article ninth, §4, of the Connecticut constitution of 1818 ("no conviction of treason, or attainder, shall work corruption of blood, or forfeiture").

In Connecticut and elsewhere in the United States, forfeiture came to be recognized, not in its common law version, which authorized the wholesale invalidation of property rights, but as an authorized adjunct for the exercise of powers specified in particular criminal statutes. 1 Bishop, Criminal Law (9th Ed. 1923) § 944.1, p. 695; 2 J. Kent, Commentaries on American Law (7th Ed. 1851) P. 464; see also note, "Bane of American Forfeiture Law—Banished at Last?" Supra, 779 n.73 and 795 n.162. Swift described Connecticut law as permitting the seizure of "a specific sum [which] is considered to be the punishment itself, and not the consequence of the judgment." 2 Z. Swift, supra. That law was exemplified by *Boles v. Lynde*, 1 Root (Conn.) 195 (1790), in which this court reviewed a conviction under a statute criminalizing fishing activity near the mouth of the Connecticut River. Any defendant convicted under the statute forfeited "the seine, ropes and other utensils used in catching fish, contrary to the act." Id. Instead of seizing the utensils, however, the trial court in *Boles v. Lynde* assessed a fine equal to the value of the fishing gear. This court reversed, holding that the property itself was subject to forfeiture, not its appraised value. See also *Ely v. Bugbee*, 90 Conn. 584, 98 A. 121 (1916) (upholding a seizure of a motor boat and eighty rods of gill net); and compare *Lawton v. Steele*, 152 U.S. 133, 139–40, 14 S. Ct. 499, 38 L. Ed. 385 (1894) (Affirming the police power of states to seize implements used in catching fish in violation of law).

While the penalty of forfeiture is therefore not "foreign" to our criminal law, we nonetheless agree with the defendant that such a sanction must be strictly construed. As a general matter, our penal law must be strictly construed to protect fundamental constitutional rights. *State v. Belton*, 190 Conn. 496, 505, 461 A.2d 973 (1983); see *United States v. Enmons*, 410 U.S. 396, 411, 93 S. Ct. 1007, 35 L. Ed. 2D 379 (1973). Forfeiture statutes in particular have been narrowly construed. *United States v. Rubin*, 559 F.2d 975, 991 (5th Cir. 1977). In applying this rule of construction, however, we must not frustrate the evident design of the legislature. *State v. Woolcock*, 201 Conn. 605, 630–31, 518 A.2d 1377 (1986).

We turn now to an application of these principles to the issue before us: Does CORA encompass the defendant's mortgage payments as "proceeds from the sale" of property illegally "acquired, maintained or used" for racketeering purposes? We conclude that CORA authorizes the state to make such property forfeitable whether or not the state can prove an intent to avoid forfeiture.

The forfeiture penalty under CORA is broad in scope. The act provides that, upon conviction, the court "shall render a judgment of forfeiture" authorizing the state to seize "all" forfeitable property. General Statutes §53-397 (b)(1). By its own terms, the act envisions the possibility of having to seize property that no longer belongs to the defendant in its original form. In such situations, the act provides two mechanisms for recapturing the property or the value thereof. If possible, "where applicable, the proceeds from the sale" of forfeitable property may be seized directly. General Statutes §53-397 (a)(1). In the alternative, the state may seek to set aside a prior fraudulent transfer under §53-397 (b)(3). Because this alternative remedy has the potential for adversely affecting innocent third parties, the court is empowered to issue appropriate orders protecting their interests. General Statutes §53-397 (b)(3).

Although the statutory scheme therefore appears, on its face, to create two unrelated and independent mechanisms for vindicating the state's right to forfeiture, the defendant urges us to construe them as interwoven. He argues that the state's right to seize "proceeds from the sale" of forfeitable property under §53-397 (a)(1) is available only upon proof that the preprosecution transfer that generated the proceeds was made with "the intention of preventing its forfeiture" as provided in §53-397 (b)(3). The "where applicable" clause in §53-397 (a)(1) is, according to the defendant, a directive to interpolate the intent requirement of §53-397 (b)(3) into the "proceeds from the sale" clause of §53-397 (a)(1). We disagree.

The set aside provision in §53-397 (b)(3) is addressed to the unique problem of recapturing "property previously owned by the defendant." (Emphasis added.) The section thereby provides a mechanism for reaching back to undo transfers that thwart the right of forfeiture. Had the defendant in this case transferred the "proceeds from the sale" of his property to a third party, the state would conceivably have a remedy under the set aside provision. That is not this case. It is undisputed that the defendant is himself receiving the mortgage payments, which clearly come within the definition of "property" in §53-394 (g). Because the defendant continues to possess the "property" that is being forfeited, this forfeiture is unaffected by §53-397(b)(3), which applies only to "property previously owned."

The absence of a specific provision relating the occurrence of forfeiture back to the commission of the offense does not, contrary to the defendant's argument, compel a different conclusion. Under the doctrine of relation back, the state may exercise a right to forfeiture as of the date of the commission of the offense, at which time ownership is said to vest in the government. *United States v. Stowell*, 133 U.S. 1, 16–17, 10 S. Ct. 244, 33 L. Ed. 555 (1890); *Florida Dealers & Growers Bank v. United States*, 279 F.2d 673, 676 (5th Cir. 1960). Under the forfeiture scheme enacted pursuant to CORA, however, this general doctrine has been superseded by a statutory framework for identifying and seizing forfeitable property. General Statutes §§53-397, 53-398.

Our conclusion that bona fide preprosecution transfers are not per se exempt from forfeiture is consistent with CORA's legislative history. In urging passage of the bill, Senator Howard T. Owens, Jr., described a hypothetical racketeer who takes a $50,000 profit gained in a cocaine transaction and invests the money in real estate, which then appreciates in value to $350,000. By subjecting the entire appreciated value of the real estate to forfeiture, he stated, "we would not allow [racketeers] to profit from their illegal activity." 25 Proc., Pt. 12, 1982 Sess., p. 3914. Further, in the House of Representatives, Representative Richard D. Tulisano stated that the forfeiture provision subjected "whatever ill gained money may be invested in, to forfeiture. There are similar laws in the federal government and some other states as well as Puerto Rico." 25 H.R. Proc., Pt. 14, 1982 Sess., p. 4540. Both statements indicate that the General Assembly intended CORA to track the progression of property "acquired, maintained and used" in illegal racketeering activity. This tracking of illicit funds occurs under federal antiracketeering law as well because its analagous purpose is to "remove the profit from organized crime by separating the racketeer from his dishonest gains." *Russello v. United States*, 464 U.S. 16, 28, 104 S. Ct. 296, 78 L. Ed. 2D 17 (1983). The trial court correctly denied the defendant's motion to discharge the CORA lien on this ground.

9.11 THE DEATH PENALTY AND THE RIGHT TO A FAIR AND SPEEDY TRIAL

Although numerous provisions of the federal criminal code and statutes of a majority of states authorize capital punishment for a variety of crimes, the actual infliction of the death penalty has steadily declined during the past years. However, the infliction of the death penalty raises substantial issues under the Eighth Amendment and the Fourteenth Amendment as well as under the Sixth Amendment with respect to the fair and speedy trial guarantees to the criminal defendant.[81] The U.S. Supreme Court in McGautha v. California[82] had expressed the difficulty of trying a capital case calling for the death penalty:

In light of history, experience, and the present limitations of human knowledge, we find it quite impossible to say that committing to the untrammeled discretion of the jury the power to pronounce life or death in capital cases is offensive to anything in the Constitution. The States are entitled to assume that jurors confronted with the truly awesome responsibility of decreeing death for a fellow human will act with due regard for the consequences of their decision and will consider a variety of factors, many of which will have been suggested by the evidence or by the arguments of defense counsel. For a court to attempt to catalog the appropriate factors in this elusive area could inhibit rather than expand the scope of consideration, for no list of circumstances would ever really be complete.

The dissenting opinion of Justice Brennan (joined by Justices Douglas and Marshall) believed that due process of law

compels the States to make explicit the fundamental policy choices upon which any exertion of State power is based, and to exercise such power only under procedures which both limit the possibility of merely arbitrary action and provide a record adequate to render meaningful the institution of federal judicial review. . . . Nothing inherent in the nature of capital sentencing . . . makes application of such procedures impossible.[83]

In 1972 in Furman v. Georgia[84] the highest court in a 5-4 vote (in five separate opinions including four separate dissents) held that the imposition and carrying out of the death penalty under an arbitrarily and randomly administered system constituted "cruel and unusual" punishment in violation of the Eighth and Fourteenth Amendments. Justice Douglas wrote that "these discretionary statutes are unconstitutional in their operation. They are pregnant with discrimination and discrimination is an ingredient not compatible with the idea of equal protection of the laws. . . . Any law which is nondiscriminatory on its face may be applied in such a way as to violate the Equal Protection Clause of the Fourteenth Amendment."[85] Indeed, the criminal defendant's right to a fair and speedy trial is jeopardized by the very "discrimination" delineated by Justice Douglas.[86]

Harsh punishment (forty years imprisonment but less than the death penalty) of a witness who refused to testify after being granted immunity was the ground for the criminal defendant's argument that he had been deprived of a fair trial in United States v. Giraldo.[87] The Second U.S. Court of Appeals found that the trial was not "infected by an apparent bias" since the acts constituting the refusal to testify and ultimate decision to testify after the sentence was imposed, took place outside the presence of the jury. Although the court was troubled by the forty-year sentence to coerce the witness to testify, the sentence did not result in a violation of the criminal defendant's right to a fair trial.

NOTES

1. See Levitt, "Jurisdiction Over Crimes," 16 J Crim L 316 (1926).
2. 188 A 574 (Penna., 1936).
3. According to the court,

In most states of the Union and under Federal authority, the constitutions fix the area within which the trial must be had or from which the jury must be empanelled. Some merely provide that the accused shall have an impartial trial or that the right of trial by jury shall remain inviolate. In the states where the constitutions expressly require the jury to be drawn from a defined area, there is a difference of opinion as to the effect of these provisions, such as the jury shall come from the "county" or "district," upon the right of the prosecutor to secure a change of venue where the accused objects. The Federal Constitution (Amendment VI) provides that the accused shall be entitled to a trial "by an impartial jury of the State and district wherein the crime shall have been committed." This amendment has been held not to be a limitation on the state courts but to apply exclusively to federal criminal procedure. . . .

"Venue" means the county or jurisdiction in which the action is brought to trial. "Vicinage," used in our Constitution, is found in few others and is of uncertain meaning. It is not coterminus with a county and may, in fact, embrace more than one county. . . . While we are not compelled, at this time, to define with exactness the extreme limits of "vicinage," enough has been said to demonstrate the trial may be removed to another county or venue, without sacrificing this constitutional guarantee.

4. "Bail is excessive when it is higher than is reasonably necessary to ensure defendant's presence at trial."
5. 479 NYS2d 738 (1st Dept., 1986).
6. See Goodman v. Kehl, 465 F2d 863 (2nd Cir., 1972).
7. People ex rel Mayor v. Commission, 500 NYS2d 684 (1st Dep., 1986).
8. Section 510.30 (2) thereof.
9. 18 USC 3041–3043, 3062, 3141–3150, 3154, 3731, 3772, and 4282 (1985). See generally 77 J of Crim L & Crim 439 (1986).
10. 18 USC 3142 (e).
11. 107 S Ct 2095 (1987).
12. 631 F Supp 1364 (SDNY, 1986).
13. 794 F2d 64 (2nd Cir., 1986).
14. Infra note 11.
15. The following cases upheld the constitutionality of the Act under the Fifth Amendment and under the Eighth Amendment: U.S. v. Zannino, 798 F2d 544 (1st Cir., 1986); U.S. v. Portes, 786 F2d 758 (7th Cir., 1986); U.S. v. Perry, 788 F2d 100 (3rd cir., 1986); U.S. v. Hazzard, 598 F Supp 1442 (ND Ill., 1984).
16. Infra note 9.
17. See 18 USC 3142 (e) and (f).

18. Id. Also, note Bell v. Wolfish, 441 US 531 (1979) setting forth the following criteria:

Whether the sanction involves an affirmative disability or restraint, whether it has historically been regarded as a punishment, whether it comes into play only on a finding of scienter, whether its operation will promote the traditional aims of punishment—retribution and deterrence, whether the behavior to which it applies is already a crime, whether an alternative purpose to which it may rationally be connected is assignable for it, and whether it appears excessive in relation to the alternative purpose assigned.

19. 790 F2d 984 (2nd Cir., 1986).
20. See Tribe, "An Ounce of Detention: Preventive Justice in the World of John Mitchell," 56 U Va L Rev 371 (1970) at 378–380.
21. See 20 U of San Fran L Rev (Winter 1986) at 319 et seq.
22. 82 Stat 1115 (1968), i.e., the Federal Magistrate Act of 1968.
23. See 18 USC appR 5 (c) (1982).
24. 93 Stat 643 (1979).
25. 18 USC 3006A (1982) and Rule 44 (a) of FRCP.
26. See 18 USC app R 1 (b) (1982).
27. 18 USC 13 (1982).
28. 352 F2d 251 (9th Cir., 1965).
29. 391 US 145 (1968).
30. _____NYS 2d_____ (Queens County, January 4, 1988).
31.

She has interviewed witnesses, and otherwise had devoted what must be over one hundred hours of detailed and exhaustive preparation of this case. Another unique fact was that Ms. Loconsolo's accident occurred on January 18, 1987, just 3 days before the subject January 21, 1987 court date. It would be absurd and unreasonable to expect the People to assign a second prosecutor to the trial of the case on such short notice. It is clear that no other A.D.A. could reasonably be expected to learn the unique facts and circumstances sufficient to prepare for Trial on any such short length of time. This is especially true when it appears that due to Ms. Loconsolo's injury, and resulting loss of short term memory, she would have been unable to brief her replacement. This is clearly "exceptional circumstances" pursuant to CPL 30.30 Subd 4 (g).

32. _____NYS2d_____ (App Div, 1st Dept., December 3, 1987).
33. 377 US 201 (1964), rev'g 307 F2d 62 (2nd Cir., 1962).
34. 360 US 315 (1959).
35. _____F Supp_____ (EDNY, Sept. 21 and Nov. 12, 1987).
36. See Kirby v. Illinois, 406 US 682 (1972).
37. Note Brewer v. Williams, 430 US 387 (1977).
38. _____F Supp_____ (SDNY, 1987).
39. _____NY2d_____ (December 17, 1987).
40. Id.

41. _____NY2d_____ (April 2, 1987).
42.

§15.20. *Effect of ignorance or mistake upon liability.* . . . 2. A person is not relieved of criminal liability for conduct because he engages in such conduct under a mistaken belief that it does not, as a matter of law, constitute an offense, unless such misbelief is founded upon an official statement of the law contained in (a) a statute or other enactment. . . . (d) an interpretation of the statute or law relating to the offense, officially made or issued by a public servant, agency, or body legally charged or empowered with the responsibility or privilege of administering, enforcing or interpreting such statute or law.

43.

The whole thrust of this exceptional exculpatory concept, in derogation of the traditional and common law principle, was intended to be a very narrow escape valve. Application in this case would invert that thrust and make mistake of law a generally applied or available defense instead of an unusual exception which the very opening words of the mistake statute make so clear, i.e., "A person is not relieved of criminal liability for conduct . . . unless . . . " (Penal Law §15.20, *supra*). The momentarily enticing argument by defendant that his view of the statute would only allow a defendant to get the issue generally before a jury further supports the contrary view because that consequence is precisely what would give the defense the unintended broad practical application.

The prosecution further counters defendant's argument by asserting that one cannot claim the protection of mistake under §15.20 (2) (a) simply by misconstruing the meaning of a statute but must instead establish that the statute relied on actually permitted the conduct in question and was only later found to be erroneous. To buttress that argument, the People analogize New York's official statement defense to the approach taken by the Model Penal Code (MPC). Section 2.04 of the MPC provides:

> Section 2.04. *Ignorance or Mistake.* (3) A belief that conduct does not legally constitute an offense is a defense to a prosecution for that offense based upon such conduct when: . . . (b) he acts in reasonable reliance upon an official statement of the law, *afterward determined to be invalid or erroneous*, contained in (i) a statute or other enactment . . . [emphasis added].

44.

In the case before us, the underlying statute never *in fact authorized* the defendant's conduct; the defendant only thought that the statutory exemptions permitted his conduct when, in fact, the primary statute clearly forbade his conduct. Moreover, by adjudication of the final court to speak on the subject in this very case, it turned out that even the exemption statute did not permit this defendant to possess the weapon. It would be ironic at best and an odd perversion at worst for this Court now to declare that the same defendant is nevertheless free of criminal responsibility.

The "official statement" component in the mistake of law defense in both subdivisions (a) and (d) adds yet another element of support for our interpretation and holding.

Defendant tried to establish a defense under Penal Law §15.20 (2) (d) as a second prong. But the interpretation of the statute relied upon must be "official made or issued by a public servant, agency or body legally charged or empowered with the responsibility or privilege of administering, enforcing or interpreting such statute or law." We agree with the People that the trial court also properly rejected the defense under Penal Law §15.20 (2) (d) since none of the interpretations which defendant proffered meets the requirements of the statute. The fact that there are various complementing exceptions to §15.20, none of which defendant could bring himself under, further emphasizes the correctness of our view which decides this case under particular statutes with appropriate precedental awareness.

45. "These are not in terrorem arguments disrespectful of appropriate adjudicative procedures; rather they are the realistic and practical consequences were the dissenters' views to prevail. Our holding comports with a statutory scheme which was not designed to allow false and diversionary stratagems to be provided for many more cases than the statutes contemplated. This would not serve the ends of justice but rather would serve game playing and evasion from properly imposed criminal responsibility."

46.

The basic difference which divides the Court may be simply put. Suppose the case of a man who has committed an act which is criminal not because it is inherently wrong or immoral but solely because it violates a criminal statute. He has committed the act in complete good faith under the mistaken but entirely reasonable assumption that the act does not constitute an offense because it is permitted by the wording of the statute. Does the law require that this man be punished? The majority says that it does and holds that (1) Penal Law §15.20 (2) (a) must be construed so that the man is precluded from offering a defense based on his mistake of law and (2) such construction is compelled by prevailing considerations of public policy and criminal jurisprudence. We take issue with the majority on both propositions.

There can be no question that under the view that the purpose of the criminal justice system is to punish blameworthiness or "choosing freely to do wrong" our supposed man who has acted innocently and without any intent to do wrong should not be punished (*see, United States v. Barker*, 514 F2d 208, 228–229, Bazelon, Ch.J., concurring). Indeed, under some standards of morality he has done no wrong at all (Patterson, Cardozo's Philosophy of Law, Part II, 88 Univ. Pa. L. Rev., pp. 169–171 [1939–1940]). Since he has not knowingly committed a wrong there can be no reason for society to exact retribution. Because the man is law-abiding and would not have acted but for his mistaken assumption as to the law, there is no need for punishment to deter him from further unlawful conduct. Traditionally, however, under the ancient rule of Anglo-American common law that ignorance or mistake of law is no excuse, our supposed man would be punished.

The dissent continued:

There are two grounds for our dissent:
    (1) that the majority's construction of Penal Law §15.20 (2) (a) is directly contrary to

the plain wording of the statute, renders the statute ineffective and deprives it of any meaning, and superimposes on the language of the statute a limitation found in the language of Model Penal Code § 2.04 (3) (b) which the Legislature has specifically rejected; and

(2) that the policy and jurisprudential reasons advanced by the majority for its rejection of what appears to be the clear intendment of Penal Law §15.20 (2) (a) are the very reasons which the Legislature has considered and rejected in its decision to abandon the unqualified common law rule in favor of permitting a limited mistake of law defense in the circumstances presented here. . . .

Any fair reading of the majority opinion, we submit, demonstrates that the decision to reject a mistake of law defense is based on considerations of public policy and on the conviction that such a defense would be bad, rather than on an analysis of CPL 15.20 (2) (a) under the usual principles of statutory construction (*see*, Majority Slip opn at 9, 10). The majority warns, for example, that if the defense were permitted "the exception would swallow the rule"; that "[m]istakes about the law would be encouraged"; that an "infinite number of mistake of law defenses . . . could be devised"; and that "wrong-minded individuals could contrive in bad faith solely to get an exculpatory motion before the jury" (Majority Slip opn. at 10).

These considerations, like the People's argument that the mistake of law defense "would encourage ignorance where knowledge is socially desired" (Respondent's Brief, p. 28), are the very considerations which have been consistently offered as justifications for the maxim "*ignorantia legis.*" That these justifications are unabashedly utilitarian cannot be questioned. It could not be put more candidly than by Justice Holmes in defending the common law maxim more than one hundred years ago: "*Public policy sacrifices the individual to the general good. . . . It is no doubt true that there are many cases in which the criminal would not have known he was breaking the law, but to admit the excuse at all would be to encourage ignorance where the lawmaker has determined to make men know and obey, and justice to the individual is rightly outweighed by the larger interest on the other side of the scales*" (Holmes, *The Common Law*, p. 48 [1881]; [emphasis added]). Regardless of one's attitude toward the acceptability of these views in the 1980's, the fact remains that the Legislature in abandoning the strict "*ignorantia legis*" maxim must be deemed to have rejected them.

We believe that the concerns expressed by the majority are matters which properly should be and have been addressed by the Legislature. We note only our conviction that a statute which recognizes a defense based on a man's good faith mistaken belief founded on a well-grounded interpretation of an official statement of the law contained in a statute is a just law. The law embodies the ideal of contemporary criminal jurisprudence "that punishment should be conditioned on a showing of subjective moral blameworthiness" (White, 77 Colum. L. Rev. 775, 784, *supra*).

It is no answer to protest that the defense may become a "false and diversionary stratagem" or that "wrong-minded individuals could contrive" an "infinite number of mistake of law defenses" (Majority Slip opn. at 10); for it is the very business of the courts to separate the true claims from the false. Such *in terrorem* arguments should have no more force here than similar objections which doubtless were voiced with equal intensity to the long-accepted defenses of justification, accident, mistake of fact, insanity, entrapment, duress and intoxication. As Justice Holmes wrote in commenting on John Austin's argument that permitting the mistake of law defense would present courts with problems they were not prepared to solve: "If justice requires the fact to be ascertained, the difficulty of doing so is no ground for refusing to try . . . (Holmes, *The Common Law*, p. 48 1881). . . .

We do not believe that permitting a defense in this case will produce the grievous consequences the majority predicts. The unusual facts of this case seem unlikely to be repeated. Indeed, although the majority foresees "an infinite number of mistake of law defenses" (Slip opn., p. 10), New Jersey, which adopted a more liberal mistake of law statute in 1978, has apparently experienced no such adversity (no case construing that law is mentioned in the most recent annotation of the statute; see, n. 8, supra, p. 11). Nor is there any reason to believe that courts will have more difficulty separating valid claims from "diversionary stratagem[s]" in making preliminary legal determinations as to the validity of the mistake of law defense than of justification or any other defense.

But that question is now beside the point, for the Legislature has given its answer in providing that someone in defendant's circumstances should have a mistake of law defense (Penal Law §15.20 [2] [a]). Because this decision deprives defendant of what, we submit, the Legislature intended that he should have, we dissent.

47. _____F2d_____ (2nd Cir., Sept. 30, 1987).
48. See Morris v. Slappy, 461 US 1 (1983).
49. See Fitzpatrick v. Procunier, 750 F2d 473 (5th Cir., 1985).
50. 744 F2d 1508 (11th Cir., 1984) at 1521.
51. Id.
52. See United States v. Coronel, 750 F2d 1482 (11th Cir., 1985), and United States v. Lehman, 756 F2d 725 (9th Cir., 1985).
53. 376 US 575 (1964).
54. Infra note 48 at 11–12.
55. See United States v. Kerris, 748 F2d 610 (11th Cir., 1984).
56. See United States v. Lehman, infra note 52 at 727–728.
57. Infra note 49 at 476–477.
58. 21 USC 848 (a)(2) (1982), 18 USC 1963(a) and (b) (1985).
59. Id.
60. Note 18 USC 1963 (a)(1) and (2) and (3) (1985); also note 21 USC 853(c) (1985).
61. 38 Crim L Rep 3001 (1985); also see Trial Magazine (September 1987) 27 et seq.
62. See United States v. Badalamenti, 614 F Supp 194 (SDNY, 1985).
63. "A lawyer shall not enter into an arrangement for, charge, or collect. . . . a contingent fee for representing a defendant in a criminal case."
64. Infra note 62.
65. 631 F Supp 1191 (ED Va., 1986), aff 814 F2d 905 (4th Cir., 1987).
66. See Powell v. Alabama, 287 US 45 (1932).
67. 644 F Supp 452 (SDNY, 1985).
68. 814 F2d 905 (4th Cir., 1987).

69. Id. at 924.
70. _____F2d_____ (2nd Cir., January 4, 1988).
71. Infra note 59.
72. _____NYS2d_____ (App Div., 2nd Dept. May 11, 1987).
73. See section 7.2 herein.
74. Infra note 63.
75. The retainer agreement read as follows:

RETAINER AGREEMENT dated this 28th day of October, 1980, by and between LANIE SATTLER, residing at One Century Tower, Fort Lee, New Jersey, and ANNIE WINKLER, residing at 1920 Scheiffelin Avenue, Bronx, New York, and [trial counsel].

WHEREAS, LANIE SATTLER desires to retain [trial counsel's law firm] to represent her son, RICHARD WINKLER, on a pending charge in Westchester County Court; and

WHEREAS, [trial counsel's law firm] agrees to accept said retainer; and

WHEREAS, ANNIE WINKLER, grandmother of RICHARD WINKLER, agrees to assist in the payment of legal fees.

NOW, THEREFORE, it is agreed as follows:

FIRST: The fee for legal representation shall be paid as follows:

(a)$2,000 on execution hereof, receipt of which is hereby acknowledged;

(b)$18,000 to be paid by ANNIE WINKLER from a bequest to be received from the Estate of Irving Winkler, at such time as said bequest is received.

SECOND: It is agreed that any disbursements for investigation or psychiatric examinations, etc., shall be in addition to the above fees.

THIRD: It is agreed that the within retainer is for the trial only, and will not include any appeals, if necessary.

FOURTH: ANNIE WINKLER has been advised and understands that in the event that RICHARD WINKLER is convicted in Westchester County Court, that she would stand to inherit the entire estate of Irving Winkler (subject to any objections by other interested parties).

FIFTH: ANNIE WINKLER agrees that said money shall be paid by her heirs, executors, administrators and assigns in the event of her death prior to payment of said fees.

SIXTH: *It is understood and agreed, subject to the approval of RICHARD WINKLER, that in the event RICHARD WINKLER is acquitted or found not guilty by reason of insanity, or some other legal reasons, and inherits from the Estate of Irving Winkler, that RICHARD WINKLER shall pay, as additional legal fees, the sum of $15,000* [emphasis added].

76.

In the case at bar, the defendant's trial counsel was obviously guilty of unprofessional and unethical conduct by entering into the aforesaid contingency fee agreement. In view of this flagrant violation of the Code of Professional Responsibility, we are forwarding a copy of our decision along with a copy of the contingency fee contract to the Grievance Committee for consideration and appropriate action. In doing so, however, we note that the fact that counsel's conduct violated a provision of the Code of Professional Responsibility does not, in and of itself, necessarily warrant a finding of ineffective assistance of counsel (see, *Morrow v. State*, 219 Kan 442, 548 P 2d 727; *Schoonover v. State*, 218 Kan 377, 543 P 2d 881, *cert denied* 424 US 944).

77.

The existence of a contingency fee agreement, such as that at bar, however, inevitably creates a real, ever present and insoluble conflict between the defendant and his or her attorney thereby threatening the sanctity of the attorney-client relationship at its very root (see, *United States v. Hurt*, 543 F 2d 162, 167). The scope and depth of the conflict created by the contingency fee agreement is substantial. The real vice of such an agreement occurs in the consideration of various strategic and tactical decisions which confront counsel throughout the trial proceedings. For example, what if before or during the trial in the case at bar, the defendant was offered a favorable plea bargain permitting him to plead guilty to a lesser included offense of manslaughter in the first or second degree? Assuming no offer of a plea bargain was made by the prosecution, should the defense counsel have initiated or attempted to initiate a discussion with a view towards obtaining a plea bargain? Would counsel be motivated to advise the defendant as to the benefits of such a bargain given the strength of the evidence against him, if in doing so, counsel would be foregoing all possibility of the contingency fee? How objective could counsel be in advising the defendant of potential defenses to second degree murder which would result in a conviction of a lesser included offense knowing that such an outcome would result in the forfeiture of the $25,000 contingency fee? The attorney's financial interest in a complete acquittal necessarily negates any motivation on counsel's part to explore a favorable plea bargain for his client or to put forth mitigating defenses which would support a conviction of a lesser included offense. Moreover, even if we were to assume that the defendant, prior to executing a contingency fee arrangement, had adamantly professed his innocence of the charged crimes to counsel and stated unequivocally that he was only interested in a complete acquittal of all charges rather than a conviction of possible lesser counts, we would still be compelled to conclude that the defendant's constitutional right to counsel was violated as a matter of law. The dynamics of a criminal case are such that the defense is frequently required to change its original trial strategy in response to various circumstances which arise during the course of the trial. As the trial progresses, for example, the prosecution's case may appear stronger than the defense originally anticipated, thereby compelling the defendant and his or her attorney to seriously reconsider their original strategy to strive for a complete acquittal of all charges and to contemplate the availability of potential mitigating defenses which, if successful, would result in a conviction of a lesser offense. Counsel's advice to the defendant regarding these tactical decisions must be unfettered, free of self-interest and directed solely towards the advancement and vindication of his or her client's legal rights and the furtherance of any opportunity that may be in the client's best interests rather than counsel's financial advancement. In contingency fee cases of this nature, however, a conflict-of-interest shadow is cast inherently over the attorney-client relationship which seriously threatens the defendant's constitutional right to meaningful, effective and unbiased legal advice from counsel. In the case at bar, for example, the defendant was constitutionally entitled to advice from his counsel, not affected in any way by the counsel's financial interest, with regard to the potential use of an intoxication defense and/or the submission of lesser included offenses to the jury. . . . In reaching this conclusion, we recognize that a number of court decisions involving contingency fee agreements in criminal cases which are relied upon by the prosecution have refused to adopt a per se rule and require a defendant to establish that actual prejudice resulted from his or her attorney's conflict of interest in order to obtain a reversal of the judgment of conviction (see, *Downs v. State*, 453 So 2d 1102 [Fla]; *Schoonover v. State*, 218 Kan 377, 543 p 2d 881, *cert denied*, 424 US 944, supra; *State v. Labonville*, 492 A 2d 1376 [NH]; *Fuller v. Israel*, 421 F Supp 582). In each of these cases, the court, following an evidentiary hearing on the defendant's motion to set aside the judgment of conviction, reviewed the defense counsel's trial performance to determine whether it met the standard of meaningful and effective legal representation required by the Sixth Amendment. Adopting this same approach, the County Court herein applied the well-established standard of review for claims of ineffective assistance of counsel set forth in *People v. Baldi* (54 NY 2d 137, supra) and determined that the defense counsel's performance at trial satisfied constitutional requirements.

See Bazelon, Questioning Authority—Justice and Criminal Law (1987), excerpted in New York Times (January 7, 1988) at B8:

We are confronted today by a class of people being left behind in an increasingly affluent society—the losers in a Hobbesian universe, a constant war of all against all and each against the other. We see them—defendants and victims—every day in our criminal justice system. Our society ignores these facts only at its peril. If we fail to acknowledge the reality of crime, if we insist on viewing defendants as mere objects to be acted upon, we will be doomed to a vicious circle of crime and repression and more crime.

Most proposals for getting tough on crime mask the painful facts and difficult choices our country must face before we can meaningfully address the crime problem. We cannot frame the issues—let alone resolve them—until we develop and consider all the relevant facts and competing considerations. . . .

Too often a false dichotomy is created between those who care about the rights of criminal defendants and those who care about victims of crime. Reality is complicated, not black and white. Most offenders and most victims share a common background, come from the same neighborhoods; where the defendant is devalued and the facts of his experience ignored, so also is the victim likely to be treated. In order to devise effective solutions to the problem, we must understand and address the problems that lead both to the criminal court. This does not require that we be blind to danger or allow criminals to prey upon us. It does require that we do not succumb to comforting slogans. . . .

Accepting the full implications of what we know about street crime might require us to provide every family with the means to create the kind of home all human beings need. It might lead us to afford the job opportunities that pose for some the only meaningful alternatives to violence. It might demand for all children a constructive education, a decent place to live, and proper pre- and postnatal nutrition. . . . More fundamentally, it might compel the eradication of racism and prejudice. . . .

78. See Hartford Courant (January 7, 1988) at B5.
79. Id.
80. 206 Conn 421 (1988).

81. See Louisiana ex rel Francis v. Resweber, 329 US 459 (1947) on the question of "cruel and unusual punishment" under the Eighth Amendment.

82. 402 US 183 (1971).

83. The dissent continued:

[E]ven if I thought these procedures adequate to try a welfare claim—which they are not, . . . —I would have little hesitation in finding them inadequate where life itself is at stake. For we have long recognized that the degree of procedural regularity required by the Due Process Clause increases with the importance of the interests at stake. Where First Amendment interests have been involved we have held the States to stringent procedural requirements indeed. Of course the First Amendment is "an interest of transcending value," but so is life itself. Yet the Court's opinion turns the law on its head to conclude, apparently, that *because* a decision to take someone's life is of such tremendous import, those who make such decisions need not be "inhibit[ed]" by the safeguards otherwise required by due process of law. My belief is to the contrary, and I would hold that no State which determines to take a human life is thereby exempted from the constitutional command that it do so only by "due process of law."

84. 408 US 238 (1972).

85. Id.

86. Note the dissent of Chief Justice Burger:

This claim of arbitrariness is not only lacking in empirical support, but it manifestly fails to establish that the death penalty is a "cruel and unusual" punishment. The Eighth Amendment was [designed] to assure that certain types of punishment would never be imposed, not to channelize the sentencing process. The approach of these concurring opinions has no antecedents in the Eighth Amendment cases. It is essentially and exclusively a procedural due process argument. Moreover, it is "plainly foreclosed" by *McGautha*, [which] sustained the prevailing system of sentencing in capital cases, finding it "impossible to say that committing to the untrammeled discretion of the jury the power to pronounce life or death in capital cases is offensive to anything in the Constitution." Although "technically" *McGautha* was confined to the dictates of due process rather than the cruel and unusual punishment prohibition, it would be disingenuous to suggest that today's ruling has done anything less than overrule *McGautha* in the guise of an Eighth Amendment adjudication.

Since the two pivotal concurring opinions turn on the assumption that the punishment of death is now meted out in a random and unpredictable manner, legislative bodies may seek to bring their laws into compliance with the Court's ruling by providing standards for juries and judges to follow in determining the sentence in capital cases or by more narrowly defining the crimes for which the penalty is to be imposed. If such standards can be devised or the crimes more meticulously defined, the result cannot be detrimental. However, Mr. Justice Harlan's opinion for the Court in *McGautha* convincingly demonstrates that all past efforts "to identify before the fact" the cases in which the penalty is to be imposed have been "uniformly unsuccessful." . . .

Real change could clearly be brought about if legislatures provided mandatory death sentences in such a way as to deny juries the opportunity to bring in a verdict on a lesser charge; under such a system, the death sentence could only be avoided by a verdict of acquittal. If this is the only alternative that the legislatures can safely pursue under today's ruling, I would have preferred that the Court opt for total abolition.

87. _____F2d_____ (2nd Cir., 1987).

10

Definitions and Terminology of Crimes

Crimes are capable of definition but unfortunately definitions vary from jurisdiction to jurisdiction, and especially internationally.[1] The definition of the crime is not only vital to the criminal defendant's defense, but is also of concern to the growing movement toward police liability for negligent failure to prevent crime.[2] Accordingly, there are certain guidelines for defining the various crimes:

Homicide is simply the death of a human being by another, but it may be non-criminal if it is justified or excused. The killer's act must be the sole or concurrent, substantial "but for" proximate cause of death, not broken by an intervening, superseding event or factor. At common law, criminal homicide was either murder or manslaughter, the former being committed with malice aforethought; and these definitions have been carried forward in state statutes. There are "degrees" of murder, first degree being associated with an intent to kill, and the second and third degrees being associated with an intent to inflict serious bodily injury with a depraved heart. However, in some jurisdictions, murder in the second degree encompasses a killing with malice aforethought but without premeditation and deliberation. Manslaughter, on the other hand, can be voluntary or non-voluntary, the former being an intentional homicide under extenuating circumstances which mitigate but do not justify or excuse the killing. Involuntary manslaughter is an unintentional homicide without malice which is not justified or excused. There is even a charge of misdemeanor-manslaughter where the killing occurred in the commission of an unlawful act not amounting to a felony; where the killing occurred during the commission of a felony, the charge is more serious and is labeled felony-murder or felony-manslaughter. Defenses to homicide include justifiable homicide which means that the killing could be authorized by law, inter alia, such as self-defense or defense of one's dwelling. Excusable homicides are homicides to which the law does not attach criminal guilt but which are not authorized by law, such as infancy, insanity, or mistake of fact.

Among the non-homicide crimes may be listed assault and battery, robbery, extortion, kidnapping, rape, as well as such little-known crimes as accessory after the fact[3] and misprision of Felony.[4] The federal conspiracy statute[5] is but another example of the myriads of non-homicide crimes. There are also crimes against property interests such as larceny, embezzlement, obtaining property by false pretenses, receiving stolen goods, burglarly, arson.

Still another category of crimes might be delineated as "inchoate crimes," i.e., attempts to commit a crime (a substantial step in the direction coupled with an intent to do so, but frustrated by an inability to commit the crime); solicitation, conspiracy, and parties to crime and accomplice liability.

Crimes are preventable, and in recent years the police have frequently been charged with liability for negligent failure to prevent crime.[6] But the majority rule seems not to recognize liability of government (sovereign immunity) or its law enforcement officers for failure to prevent crime, unless there is shown a special relationship between the police and the victim.[7] In Schuster v. City of New York[8] the New York Court of Appeals held that the police could be liable for failure to provide adequate protection to a citizen who was murdered for aiding them in the arrest of a fugitive: "The public (acting in this instance through the City of New York) owes a special duty to use reasonable care for the protection of persons who have collaborated with it in the arrest or prosecution of criminals, once it reasonably appears that they are in danger due to their collaboration.[9] There are innumerable similar cases of police liability for failure to protect persons abetting the police as informers or witnesses.[10] In Jones v. County of Herkimer[11] the New York court imposed liability because of the assailant's previous conviction for assaulting the person he later killed; a special relationship existed requiring the police to provide reasonable protection to the victim, which the police negligently failed to do. But police owed no duty to victims of drunken driving when the police failed to arrest the offender.[12]

The federal government, on the other hand, has been practically immune from liability for its negligent failure to prevent crime, probably due to the many obstacles set forth in the Federal Tort Claims Act.[13] The "discretionary function" exception is generally applied to crime prevention activity, and the federal agencies simply do not respond in damages.[14]

Section 1983 of the Civil Rights Act,[15] on the other hand, provides federal relief for victims of police failure to prevent crimes because the Section reaches the conduct of state and local law enforcement officers and officials.[16] Section 1983 triggers the deprivation of many constitutional rights including the right to a fair and speedy trial.

International criminal law devolves about the individual and is not necessarily an indirect subject of international law.[17] Among the international criminal offenses is piracy,[18] which every state is entitled to prosecute and punish. This crime consists of an illegal act of violence, detention, or depredation which is committed from a ship or aircraft other than the one serving as a target of the offense; piracy occurs on the high seas or in the air or outside the jurisdiction of states. War crimes constitute grave offenses against laws of war.[19] Crimes against humanity is another category of crime encompassing murder, extermination, enslavement, deportation and other inhumane acts committed against civilian populations.[20] Genocide is the crime of intentionally destroying a national, ethnical, racial, or religious group of people.[21] Other international crimes include apartheid, racial discrimination, enslavement and slave trade, torture, narcotic drug transactions, traffic in prostitution, aircraft hijacking, counterfeiting of currency, destruction or interference with submarine cables, aircraft sabotage, and terrorism.[22] The fundamental rights of fair and speedy trial are part and parcel of any trial for these international crimes under the Universal Declaration of Rights of Man and other international legislation.[23]

In delineating definitions and terminology of crimes, more than a passing reference must be made to (a) crime victim's rights, and (b) rights of the unjustly convicted. The former is the subject of a new tort, i.e., the failure of the government to protect such victims as when the police fail to respond or intervene when the police know or should have known that someone is in peril.[24] In Thurman v. City of

Torrington[25] a battered wife had a constitutional cause of action against the police for police refusal to respond to her repeated calls for assistance and for police inaction while her estranged husband assaulted her. And in Nishiyama v. Dickson County[26] the Sixth U.S. Court of Appeals upheld a federal civil rights case based upon a county sheriff allowing a prisoner to run errands, the prisoner then raping and murdering, while he was free. Even landlords have a duty to protect their tenants from criminal harm, as illustrated by Kline v. 1500 Massachusetts Avenue Apartment Corp.[27] A tenant, raped in her apartment, stated a cause of action in negligence against her landlord.[28] Hospitals also have been held liable for failure to provide adequate security for patients, staff, and employees.[29] On the defense are the traditional tort doctrines of sovereign immunity[30] and lack of proximate cause.

As to the rights of the unjustly convicted the New York case of Moses v. State of New York[31] is illustrative; here the court dealt with the benefits under the New York Unjust Conviction and Imprisonment Act of 1984.[32] The plaintiff was convicted of felony-murder and third degree robbery, but on appeal, the New York Court of Appeals[33] reversed and dismissed the indictment, holding that a false alibi was the only evidence corroborating a witness's testimony. Plaintiff thereupon unsuccessfully sued under the Act for his twenty-two months imprisonment, and the State of New York defended on the ground that plaintiff had failed to satisfy the pleading specificity required under the Act,[34] and furthermore that his false alibi disqualified him from relief under the Act. The court opined:

In enacting the statute, the Legislature struck a balance between the competing goals of compensating those unjustly convicted and imprisoned and preventing the filing of frivolous claims by those who are not actually innocent (see, 1984 Report of NY Law Rev Commn [Report], at 2926). To avoid overburdening the representatives of the State, detailed pleading requirements were adopted to enable the culling out of meritless actions as early in the proceeding as possible. (Id.) In fact, it was anticipated that few claims would survive a motion to dismiss. (Id., at 2930).

Of course, within this framework, the actual specificity required must be a sui generis determination based on the particular situation presented. In rare circumstances, a reversal itself may sufficiently establish innocence as to dispense with further pleadings or proof. (Cf., Reed v. State of New York, ___ AD2d____, 518 NYS2d 645). Where the reason for the dismissal is equivocal, other evidence must be submitted. While it need not be documentary (Dozier v. State of New York, _____AD2d_____, Nov. 19, 1987), allegations must be factual and of such a character that if believed would clearly and convincingly establish the elements of the claim. . . .

Here, the Court of Appeals' reversal was based solely on the technical ground that the testimony of the prosecution's key witness was insufficiently corroborated. That court neither found nor intimated that claimant was actually innocent. Moreover, while the trial court feared that Moses might be innocent, that it is a far cry from establishing his innocence by clear and convincing evidence.

Clear and convincing evidence is a standard which is higher and more demanding than by a mere preponderance (Rossi v. Hartford Fire Ins. Co., 103 AD2d 771; 4 Bender's NY Evidence §184.02; Fisch, NY Evidence §1090), and is not satisfied by evidence which is "loose, equivocal or contradictory (George Backer Mgt. Corp. v. Acme Quilting Co., 46 NY2d 211, 220; see, Chimart Assoc. v. Paul, 66 NY2d 570, 574). Justice Dontzin's concern that claimant might be innocent is equivocal at best. Moreover, claimant abandoned that theory on appeal and the Appellate Division reversed.

Thus, on the papers before us, we cannot find that claimant is likely to succeed at trial in proving his innocence by clear and convincing proof. The judicial pronouncements only raise questions rather than answering them and claimant has offered no additional factual support as might warrant a trial. While questions of witness credibility should not generally be decided on papers, twelve of his peers have already found claimant guilty beyond a reasonable doubt and his conviction was overturned solely on a technical ground not available in this civil proceeding (Fudgar v. State of New York, AD2d [Oct. 29, 1987]; see, Report, at 2929; accord, United States v. Brunner, 200 F2d 276 [6th Cir., 1952]). In light thereof, more than a one sentence assertion of innocence is required to satisfy the pleading requirements of the statute and justify a trial.

In addition, to be eligible for relief, Moses must show that "he did not by his own conduct cause or bring about his conviction (Court of Claims Act §8-b [4 (b)]). The purpose of this requirement is to ensure that a claimant is not rewarded for his own misconduct (Report, at 2932).

In its Report, the Law Revision Commission cited five examples of types of misconduct that would bar relief. These include giving an uncoerced confession of guilt, removing evidence, attempting to induce a witness to give false testimony, attempting to suppress testimony or concealing the guilt of another (Id.; see, e.g., Stevenson v. State of New York, _____ Misc 2d _____, 520 NYS2d 492).

Claimant objects that offering a false alibi is not one of the proscribed activities. As is readily apparent, the list is only illustrative and not exhaustive. If it were to be limited to the five items specified, there would be no need to characterize them as examples. Moreover, while the issue is one of first impression in this jurisdiction, our interpretation is supported by the case law under 28 USC §2513, the Federal unjust conviction and imprisonment statute, upon which section 8-b was based in part (see, Report at 2920; compare 28 USC §2513 with Court of Claims Act §8-b).

NOTES

1. See Dinstein, "International Criminal Law," 20 Israel L Rev (1985) at 206 et seq.
2. See 94 Harv L Rev 821 (1981).
3. Note 18 USC 3, for example: "Whoever, knowing that an offense against the United States has been committed, receives, relieves, comforts or assists the offender in order to hinder or prevent his apprehension, trial or punishment, is an accessory after the fact." The assistance given must be to a felon, known by the accessory to have committed a felony. See United States v. Day, 533 F2d 524 (10th Cir., 1976).
4. Note 18 USC 4, for example: "Whoever, having knowledge of the actual commission of a felony cognizable by a court of the United States, conceals and does not as soon as possible make known the same to some judge or other person in civil or military authority under the United States, shall be fined not more than $500 or imprisoned no more than three years, or both." See United States v. Johnson, 546 F2d 1225 (5th Cir., 1977) to the effect that mere failure to report the crime was insufficient to constitute misprision; there must be some affirmative act of concealment.
5. Note 18 USC 371:

If two or more persons conspire either to commit an offense against the United States, or to defraud the United States, or any agency thereof in any manner or for any purpose, and one or more of such persons do any act to effect the object of the conspiracy, each shall be fined not more than $10,000 or imprisoned not more than five years, or both.
The elements of the offense of conspiracy are:
First: That two or more persons, in some way or manner, came to a mutual understanding to try to accomplish a common and unlawful plan . . . ;
Second: That the Defendant willfully became a member of the conspiracy;
Third: That one of the conspirators during the existence of the conspiracy knowingly committed at least one of the methods (or "overt acts") described in the indictment; and
Fourth: That such "overt act" was knowingly committed at or about the time alleged in an effort to carry out or accomplish some object of the conspiracy.

6. Infra note 2.
7. See Hartzler v. City of San Jose, 120 Cal Rptr 5 (1975).

8. 5 NY2d 75, 154 NE2d 534 (1958).
9. Id. at 80-81 and at 537.
10. See Swanner v. United States, 309 F Supp 1183 (MD Ala., 1970), and Christy v. City of Baton Rouge, 282 So2d 724 (La App., 1973).
11. 272 NYS2d 925 (1966).
12. See Wuethrich v. Delia, 382 A2d 929 (N.J., 1978).
13. 28 USC 1346(b) and 2674 (1976).
14. See Smith v. United States, 375 F2d 243 (5th Cir., 1967), cert den 389 US 841 (1967).
15. 42 USC 1983 (1976) reads as follows:

Every person who, under color of any statute, ordinance, regulation, custom, or usage, of any State or Territory, subjects, or causes to be subjected, any citizen of the United States or other person within the jurisdictin thereof to the deprivation of any rights, privileges, or immunities secured by the Constitution and laws, shall be liable to the party injured in an action at law, suit in equity, or other proper proceeding for redress.

16. See Monell v. Department of Social Services, 436 US 658 (1978).
17. Infra note 1 at 206.
18. Note 52 AM J Internat L 842 (1958) and 21 ILM 1261 and 1288–1289 (1982).
19. See Dinstein, The Laws of War (1983).
20. Infra note 1 at 210.
21. Id. at 212:

The term "genocide" was coined by Lemkin against the background of the Holocaust, and is based on a combination of the Greek word *genos* (meaning race or tribe) with the Latin radical—*cidium* (meaning killing, as, for instance, in patricide). In 1948, the General Assembly of the United Nations adopted a Convention on the Prevention and Punishment of the Crime of Genocide. The Convention defines genocide in Art. 11 as any of the following acts committed with intent to destroy—in whole or part—a national, ethnical, racial or religious group, as such: (a) killing members of the group; (b) causing serious bodily or mental harm to members of the group; (c) inflicting on the group conditions of life calculated to bring about its physical destruction; (d) imposing measures intended to prevent births within the group; or (e) forcibly transferring children of the group to another group.

22. Infra note 1.
23. See Warren Freedman, The International Human Right to Travel (Martinus Nijhoff, 1988).
24. See Trial Magazine (January 1988) at 79 et seq.
25. 595 F Supp 1521 (Conn., 1984).
26. 814 F2d 277 (6th Cir., 1987).
27. 439 F2d 477 (DC Cir., 1970).
28. See Lay v. Dworman, 732 P2d 455 (Okla., 1987).

29. See Small v. McKennan Hospital, 403 NW2d (S.D., 1987).

30. See Chapter 10 of Warren Freedman, International Products Liability (2 vol., 1987).

31. New York Ct of Claims, January 20, 1988.

32. New York Laws 1984, Ch 1009, adding Section 8-b of Court of Claims Act.

33. 63 NY2d 299 (1986).

34. Section 8-b(4) of the Court of Claims Act provides:

The claim shall state *facts in sufficient detail* to permit the court to find that claimant is likely to succeed at trial in proving that (a) he did not commit any of the acts charged in the accusatory instrument or his acts or omissions charged in the accusatory instrument did not constitute a felony or misdemeanor against the state, and (b) he did not by his own conduct cause or bring about his conviction. The claim shall be verified by the claimant. If the court finds after reading the claim that claimant is not likely to succeed at trial, it shall dismiss the claim, either on its own motion or on the motion of the state.

Bibliography

Brill, "Inside the DeLorean Jury Room," Am Law 1, 99 (December 1984).
Frederick, "Jury Behavior: A Psychologist Examines Jury Selection," 5 Ohio N U L Rev 571 (1978).
Frederick, "Voir Dire and Peremptory Challenges," Cases & Comment (Jan–Feb 1988) at 18 et seq.
Ginger, Jury Selection in Criminal Trials (1980).
Hogan, M. R., "Drawing the Line on Civil Rights Fees," THE BRIEF Magazine (Winter 1988) at 11 et seq.
Newberg, "Decision Affects Enhancements Required in Statutory Fee Awards," NLJ (Feb. 22, 1988) at 18 et seq.
Note, "Unjust Convictions, Imprisonment Claims," NYLJ (Jan. 28, 1987) at 1 et seq.
Note, "Voir Dire—A View from the Defense," NYLJ (May 5, 1983) at 1 et seq.
Silverman, "Survey of the Law of Peremptory Challenges: Uncertainty in the Criminal Law," 44 U Pitt L Rev (Spring 1983) at 675.
Starr, "The Shifting Panorama of Attorneys' Fees Awards: The Expansion of Fee Recoveries in Federal Court," 28 S Tex L Rev 189 (1986).
6 Whiteman, Digest of International Law 736 (1968).

Index to Cases

174   Index to Cases

Subject Index

ABOUT THE AUTHOR

WARREN FREEDMAN was formerly General Counsel for Bristol Myers. His previous books include *Foreign Plaintiffs in Products Liability Actions, Frivolous Lawsuits and Frivolous Defenses, Federal Statutes on Environmental Protection, The Right of Privacy in the Computer Age,* and *Professional Sports and Antitrust.*